The Home
of Infinite
Possibilities

Gary M. Douglas
and **Dr. Dain Heer**

Published by
Access Consciousness Publishing, LLC
www.accessconsciousnesspublishing.com

Printed in the United States of America
Ease, Joy and Glory

The kind of change we would like to see in the world is where judgment, vilification, and abuse no longer exist, and a different world is possible. This is what infinite possibilities are about.

Dr. Dain Heer

Foreword

In the winter of 2015, Dr. Dain Heer and I hosted a two-day class called Home of Infinite Possibilities, in which we talked with class participants about the magnanimous nature of the universe, the power of committing to your life, the perils of buying into this reality, and many other things including relationships, kids, money, and the fire-breathing dragon of possibility called YOU.

This book is based on those conversations and it contains many of the clearings we did using the Access Consciousness Clearing Statement®. The clearing statement goes like this:

Right and Wrong, Good and Bad, POD and POC, All 9, Shorts, Boys, and Beyonds.®

If you've never encountered the clearing statement before, it may twist your head around a little bit. That's our intention. It's designed to get your mind out of the picture so you can get to the energy of a situation and clear the limitations and barriers that keep you from moving forward and expanding into the spaces you'd like to go. There is information about the clearing statement, what the words mean, and how it works at the end of this book and at http://www.theclearingstatement.com

You can choose to use the clearing statement or not; we don't have a point of view about that, but we invite you to try it and see what happens.

Gary M. Douglas

Table of Contents

1
The Home of Infinite Possibilities

Dain:

Gary and I are hoping to dislodge the absolute necessity in your world to choose a small, limited, painful life and instead choose to make your life about infinite possibilities and infinite choice. And there's something we want to let you know about choosing this: It never looks the way you think it will. Just remember that a few months from now.

Gary:

Later when you look at what showed up, you'll realize, "Oh! This is even greater than what I wanted!" That's because when you are functioning from infinite possibilities, the smallest part of you is no longer the one in charge. Infinite possibilities show up when you allow yourself to be in the natural flow of the magnanimous universe and to have the ease of that. Most people don't allow this. They could choose total ease, total joy, total glory, total possibilities, riches, wealth, and health, but instead they choose a small, limited life.

The home of infinite possibilities is where you choose from possibility, where you create from possibility, and where you have infinite possibility.

In this reality, we aren't taught about infinite possibility; instead, we get indoctrinated into the finite possibility of this reality. We are told, "You can't do that. You can't have that. Things can't be that way."

It's sad but true. Throughout my life people have told me, "What you want is just not possible. Life's not that easy. You can't have it that good." My question has always been: "Why not?"

People would tell me, "This is what you should choose. This is what you should do. This is the way it is supposed to be." I'd say, "That can be your reality. I don't like your reality. I am going to have a different one."

A friend said that when he was a kid, every time he wanted something greater, his parents would ask him, "Who do you think you are that you can have that? Who do you think you are that you can do that?" Those questions were intended to do what? To get him to choose less. To indoctrinate him into the finite possibility of this reality.

> *Throughout my life people have told me,*
> *"What you want is just not possible.*
>
> *Life's not that easy. You can't have it that good."*
> *My question has always been: "Why not?"*

COLORING OUTSIDE THE LINES

Gary:

When you were little, did you color outside the lines in your coloring books? You probably didn't see a problem with coloring outside the lines, but the adults kept trying to teach you to stay inside them. Everything was about staying inside the lines, and that's what became real to you.

Dain:

I recently got a thank-you card from Gary's three-year-old grandson Zander. His mom was getting him to write thank-you cards. The card has little dinosaurs printed on it, and Zander had drawn all over them with a crayon. It's a perfect example of the way you ought to be: "There are lines here—screw that!" The card says, "I love you. Thank you," and on the back in his Mom's very nice handwriting is all the stuff Zander would have said had he thought about saying it.

Have you created your life as something to be lived inside the lines? Would you like to let go of living within the lines and start becoming un-linear? Everything that is, would you destroy and uncreate it? Right and Wrong, Good and Bad, POD and POC, All 9, Shorts, Boys, and Beyonds.

Gary:

When we were talking about coloring outside the lines in the Home of Infinite Possibilities class, someone said, "I love being outside the lines and coloring outside the lines, yet when I sneak outside the lines, I get the feeling that the other shoe is going to drop."

I asked, "Do you realize that you are not choosing the possibilities in your life? You are only sneaking them in under the cover of darkness."

Everything you have done to sneak possibility into your life instead of choosing it, will you destroy and uncreate it all? Right and Wrong, Good and Bad, POD and POC, All 9, Shorts, Boys, and Beyonds.

"There are lines here—screw that!"

HOW HAVE YOU CREATED YOUR LIFE?

Gary:

Do you align and agree with this reality? Do you try to fit into this reality? Yes, you do, at least sometimes. Trying to fit into this reality means trying to align and agree with it. You say, "I am going to fit in." "I must fit in." "I do not fit it in." You ask, "How do I fit in? What is wrong with me that I don't fit in?" You are committed to this reality. You figure that since everybody else is doing something, you should be doing it, too. But just because everyone is jumping off the cliff does not mean that you should jump off the cliff as well.

Dain:

You jump of the cliff and you go "splat" then you run to the top of the cliff to do it again. You say, "Everybody is doing it, so come on, let's go!" You do not recognize that the reality beyond this reality is space. There is no solidity to it.

Gary:

It is the space of possibilities.

Dain:

It's like there is a blue haze, which is the space of possibilities, and it is all around everybody—but nobody sees it. You see it and you say, "I want to tap into the blue haze."

Other people say, "What blue haze?"

You say, "Wait! Feel it. Do you perceive it?"

They say, "Nope! I am going to jump off the cliff again. You are missing your place in line."

Gary:

Why are you not being a leader who goes forward whether anybody goes with you or not? If nobody came to Access, I would still move forward with consciousness. I would still be working on consciousness every day. I'd be asking:

- How can I be more aware here?
- How many more possibilities are there?
- What else can I choose that I have not chosen?

Those are the places I live every day.

You have the idea that there is something to this reality, that there is something to fit into, that there is a going home, that there is a place where you belong. What if it was not about the *place* you *belong* but the *space* you *are*?

> **You do not recognize that the reality**
> **beyond this reality is space.**

YOU, THE INFINITE BEING

Gary:

Infinite possibility is about being everything you are. You have to commit to being the infinite *you*. Dain and I were talking with a lady who wanted to know how she could describe herself as the infinite being she truly is. She said, "I don't know whether

I'm choosing to be vague—or whether there's nothing there to describe."

Dain:

I said, "You may have the sense that if something is not solid and you cannot touch it, that nothing is there. That is not so. It's just that there is nothing solid enough to be called you."

Gary:

I said, "It's about the energy you have to be."

She said, "But sometimes there seems to be a requirement that I use words to give people that."

Gary:

I said, "All you have to do is ask: 'What can this person hear?' and you'll know the words you need to say. You are trying to explain what is true for you rather than asking, 'What can this person hear?' You could ask: 'What is the energy I have to be to create whatever I desire with total ease?'"

> **You may have the sense that if something
> is not solid and you cannot touch it that
> nothing is there. That is not so.**
>
> **It's just that there is nothing solid
> enough to be called you.**

YOU CAN'T SEE POSSIBILITIES BUT YOU CAN BE AWARE OF THEM

Gary:

There are things that exist which you cannot see. You are one of them. It's the same with possibilities. In a facilitators' class many moons ago, we talked about seeing the possibilities and seeing the future. A class participant whose father was a scientist said she was taught, "If you can't see it, it's not real," thus, infinite possibilities couldn't be real because we can't see them.

We try to *see* the future and we can't. We try to *see* possibilities and we can't, so we conclude they don't exist. That is a mistake. We can't *see* them—but we can *be aware* of them. *Seeing* is less than one godzillion percent of what *awareness* would tell us.

Do you ever see something as it really is? Or do you see it through your judgments and your points of view? You only see it through your judgments and points of view. You can't even see all of *you.* Can you see *you* in the mirror? No, the mirror is the reflection of your judgments; it is not a reflection of what actually is.

We try to see possibilities and we can't, so we conclude they don't exist—but we can *be aware* of them. We can perceive the energy of them. And we can receive them.

Seeing is less than one godzillion percent of what awareness would tell us.

BEING, PERCEIVING, KNOWING, AND RECEIVING

Dain:

Seeing is always jaded by our points of view, our judgments, and the judgments we are buying from everybody else that we aren't even aware of. *Perceiving* is simply recognizing what is. It has no judgment or value attached. It's "Oh, that person is selfish. No big deal; he's selfish. Now I know."

If you go to seeing rather than perceiving, you'll try to see that person as perfect or you'll try to see why he is selfish. You'll try to see a reason and a justification for his selfishness rather than simply perceiving, "Oh, okay. He is selfish."

Gary:

Or you'll try and see how bad he is for being selfish. That is where you try to use your judgment as a weapon and a tool against being present in your own life.

Dain:

It is the *being*, not the seeing. It is the *perceiving*, the *knowing*, and the *receiving* that enable us to realize that the universe is magnanimous and possibilities are infinite.

Seeing *is always jaded by our point of view. Perceiving is simply recognizing what is.*

2
The Universe Is Magnanimous

Gary:

The universe wishes to support us, but we act like we are all alone. It's as if we think the universe is an ecosystem we have to exclude ourselves from. We think we have to do everything ourselves because we don't realize that we are part of a whole. Why do we do that? I don't have an answer. But I do know we create a lot of stupidity to make sure we don't receive what the universe wishes to gift us.

The magnanimous universe is the place where the universe has our back and takes care of us. It's where everything in life tries to contribute to us, but we refuse that contribution.

If we embrace ourselves as part of the whole universe without any judgment, we invite it to be part of us and we open to it, which gives us everything we desire. With every question, every choice, and every possibility, we invite the quantum entanglements of the entire universe to join with us to actualize what we desire.

Dain:

The universe never ceases to give to us. It never says, "You didn't make your bed so I'm not going to give you anything today. You're a bad person. You need to sit in your dirty diapers." The universe never does that.

The trees don't say, "I'm not going to give you any oranges because you're a jerk." They say, "Okay, you're a jerk. Here are some oranges. Maybe these will help you out." That's how magnanimous the universe is. It never has a whiff of judgment.

THE MAGNANIMOUS UNIVERSE IS YOUR TRUE HOME

Dain:

Magnanimous means generous in forgiving insult or injury; unselfish. The opposite of magnanimous is *penurious*, which means extremely stingy; miserly; poverty stricken. We live in a magnanimous universe that gifts to us all the time, but we choose to live a reality that tells us the magnanimous universe doesn't exist.

How much energy are you using to create the penurious reality as your reality rather than the magnanimous universe as your universe of possibilities are you choosing? Everything that is, will you destroy and uncreate it all? Right and Wrong, Good and Bad, POD and POC, All 9, Shorts, Boys, and Beyonds.

Gary:

The magnanimous universe is your true home. People's slights or their judgments don't have any effect on you when you're functioning from the magnanimous universe. They're like water off a duck's back.

The universe always delivers exactly what you ask for. If you are not getting what you desire and would like to have in your life, it is because you are not asking the universe for that.

Dain:

It is not because the universe is broken or does not like you.

Gary:

The consciousness that exists on this planet, in this world, and in this universe is magnanimous. The magnanimous universe is the place where the universe has our back. It takes care of us. It doesn't judge us. If you're not willing to have how magnanimous the universe is, then you must believe in judgment—and not possibilities.

We live in a magnanimous universe that gifts to us all the time, but we choose to live a reality that tells us that the magnanimous universe doesn't exist.

ARE YOU WILLING TO RECEIVE WHAT YOU DESIRE?

Gary:

The universe functions with total kindness and total generosity from the consciousness it is. It never functions with judgment of anyone or anything. It never judges anything you choose. It is a magnanimous universe that is infinitely gifting, yet we seldom ask for what we desire, and that which we ask for, we are seldom willing to receive. We keep saying, "I just can't have it. I just can't do it."

You cut off the universe from contributing to you when you try to control how you receive. The universe likes you better than you like yourself and it wishes to contribute far more to you than you are willing to receive. In order to receive what the magnanimous universe gives us, we have to be willing to have a level of receiving that comes from possibilities.

Have you given up receiving, thinking that is the way you have to be because that is what this reality tells you? Everything that is times a godzillion, will you destroy and uncreate it all? Right and Wrong, Good and Bad, POD and POC, All 9, Shorts, Boys, and Beyonds.

Dain:

When you ask for something, you don't allow yourself to receive it because you don't realize we live in a magnanimous universe.

Gary:

The universe will give you exactly what you ask for.

Dain:

You could say, "I'd really like to have greater possibilities in my life."

Gary:

Or you could ask: "How does it get any better than this?"

Dain:

Or you could ask:

- What else is possible?
- How can we have more fun than this?
- How can I enjoy today more than I've ever enjoyed any other day in the past?

Gary:

What have you made so vital about never totally possessing the gift that the magnanimous universe wishes to give you that keeps you from having the ease of life you could be choosing? Everything that is times a godzillion, will you destroy and uncreate it all? Right and Wrong, Good and Bad, POD and POC, All 9, Shorts, Boys, and Beyonds.

The universe would like to contribute far more
to you than you are willing to receive.

3
The Power of Committing to Your Life

Gary:

It's no surprise that we grow up thinking that life is hard and possibilities do not exist—because no one has taught us about being, perceiving, knowing, and receiving. We have never been educated about how to be on this planet, and when we are not educated about something, we do not realize that it is part of what we need. That's why we talk so much in Access classes about how to choose from consciousness.

Dain:

We have never been educated about how to choose infinite possibilities. It is something we have never been given. A lot of us were never even educated about how to handle our lives. My parents never taught me, like some people's parents taught them, how to do some of the basics in the world: how to write letters or address envelopes or send thank-you notes. I didn't learn how to organize things, how to file, or how to balance a checkbook. Balancing my checkbook was important enough to me personally that I figured it out, but I was never educated about it.

Gary:

Did you have parents who taught you how to actually handle money? Or was the sum total of your education "Do not spend it?" "Do not spend it" is not how to handle money. That is how to not get rid of it.

A friend said, "When I was a kid I was never taught anything. As an adult I had to figure out things like 'Oh, taking stuff that belongs to other people is considered stealing.' I didn't get that. I don't feel that I was educated on how to be on this planet—except by watching television." We're actually a lot like my friend. We have never been educated about how to be on this planet, much less how to choose infinite possibilities.

> **No one has taught us about being,
> perceiving, knowing, and receiving.**

CREATING A BIG LIFE

Gary:

Were you not educated about how to create your life, let alone how to create a big life?

You weren't, were you? You were educated to fit into the smallest box possible so people could keep you under their thumb. That way, they knew where you were. They could define who you were, and as long as you were definable and confinable, they could find you. They never wanted you to make your life so big that you could not be found according to their reality.

So how do you create a big life? The key is making a commitment to your life. When you commit to your life, you begin to realize what you are and what you can be. You begin to see that you can create *you* as the gift, *you* as the possibility, and *you* as the inspiration for a different reality. Most people are not willing to do that. They will commit themselves to others and they will commit themselves to doing things, but committing to your life is a whole different universe.

What do people teach you here in this reality? How to *be*? Or how to *not be*? They teach you how to *not be*. They teach you how to *do* but they never teach you how to *be*. If you don't come to Access, you don't learn how to *be*. That's shocking to me.

When you commit to your life, you are willing to be, do, have, create, and generate anything in order to have your life. If money is part of your life, you will be willing to be, do, have, create, and generate anything to get it. But as long as you are not committed to your life, you do not have to have money, which means you do not have the freedom to never have to rely on anybody else again.

> **When you commit to your life, you begin to realize what you are and what you can be.**

ARE YOU COMMITTED TO YOUR LIFE? OR ARE YOU COMMITTED TO LEAVING?

Gary:

We don't commit to our lives because we're living with our back door open. We leave our back door open so when things don't show up as we would like—when we don't have enough clients, when the money isn't showing up, when there's a problem in our relationship—we can leave. We can quit or we can threaten to quit. We can slide out the back door.

Plan A is committing to your life. Do you choose Plan A? Or do you have a Plan B in your relationship or your business? That Plan B is your back door. What would it be like to close the back door and fully commit to your life?

Dain:

We're always looking for a reason and a justification for leaving. We're looking for what we can choose and what we can do so we can leave ourselves.

Gary:

What is the power you have given to leaving and being left? Being left is cool because that means the other person has power and you have no choice. You say, "I have been left. How pathetic am I?" You think the power is to leave before you get left. I like that one. When people tell me they're upset about somebody leaving them, I ask, "So when did *you* leave the relationship?" It is usually several years before they got to the end of it. One lady told me she had left the relationship six months before she got married. Oops. You have already left but you are getting married anyway? That's not too bright. When did *you* leave that created *the other person* leaving?

People say, "I got fired. Oh my God, I lost my job!"

I'll ask, "Well, did you really want that job?"

They say, "Well, actually, no."

I'll say, "That is why you lost it. You had already left the job."

When did you actually leave the thing you are mourning that you lost? Everything that is times a godzillion, will you destroy and uncreate it all? Right and Wrong, Good and Bad, POD and POC, All 9, Shorts, Boys, and Beyonds.

Do you get how much unconsciousness is attached to the commitment to leave? People think there is power in leaving, but the power is actually in: "I *can* leave, but I am *not* leaving."

Death is one of the many ways we leave that does not create power because once we die, we have to come back and wear diapers. You die so you do not have to wear a diaper so you can come back and wear diapers.

Dain:

Maybe we can create a class on dying consciously called Death and Then Diapers.

People think that "F--k you" and the power to leave are the only power they have.

How committed are you to the "F--k you" you are waiting to choose, to leave your own life? Everything that is times a godzillion, will you destroy and uncreate it, please? Right and Wrong, Good and Bad, POD and POC, All 9, Shorts, Boys, and Beyonds.

Gary:

What have you made so vital about the commitment to leaving and threatening to leave that keeps you from the joy of committing to your life?

Dain:

If you're not truly present and committed to your life, how can you be happy?

Gary:

If you're sad, it's because you've got your back door open. Close your frigging back door!

If you feel like you don't have the ability to commit to your own life, there's some part of what you have as a capacity that you're not acknowledging. When you can acknowledge that, this can change and you can choose.

You may think that committing to your life is something that somebody else is trying to get you to do. But we're asking you to commit to your own life *for you.* We're asking you to get to the place where you say, "I'm not leaving *for me.* I'm not sliding out through the back door *for me.* This is not something that I will do."

What would you have to acknowledge about you that you've never acknowledged about you that if you did would give you the ability to commit to your own life and create infinite possibilities? Everything that is times a godzillion, will you destroy and uncreate it all? Right and Wrong, Good and Bad, POD and POC, All 9, Shorts, Boys, and Beyonds.

> *People think there is power in leaving,*
> *but the power is actually in: "I can*
> *leave, but I am not leaving."*

WHEN YOU COMMIT TO YOUR LIFE, YOU GIVE UP YOUR BACK DOOR

Gary:

When you're not committed to your life, it is hard for your business to grow. The reason is that you are *doing* instead of *being*. When you commit to your life, suddenly the business starts to turn in a different direction. Impossible things start to fall into place. Things you have been ignoring or avoiding or thinking couldn't be changed suddenly change. You look at all the things that seemed impossible and you ask, "Why did I think that was not possible?"

When you commit to your life, you give up your back door. Do you realize there are places and spaces in your business where you are excluding something or someone as a way of making sure you have a way to leave?

Dain:

You're trying to make sure you don't have to connect completely with *you*. Let's say a certain person is aware; they see

28

and perceive this aspect of you. You don't want to perceive that aspect of who you are, because it's the thing that would make you stay and commit to your own life—so you think you have to separate from that person. You think you have to separate from the awareness they have about you.

You say to the person, "I will let you come this close, but that's it, because if you see this aspect of me, I can't keep my facade in place." Most of us spend our entire lives holding in place a major facade about things, as a way of not committing to our own lives and keeping our back door open.

Who or what are you that you claim not to be that if you would be it would give you all of you and infinite possibilities? Everything that is times a godzillion, will you destroy and uncreate it all? Right and Wrong, Good and Bad, POD and POC, All 9, Shorts, Boys, and Beyonds.

Who or what are you that you claim not to
be that if you would be it would give you
all of you and infinite possibilities?

OPENING THE DOORS TO EVERYTHING YOU'RE CAPABLE OF

Gary:

You are always looking for your power and what you are capable of, and all it takes is making a commitment to your life. When you choose to commit to your life, you open the doors to everything you are capable of. Suddenly a different universe opens up. People become willing to contribute to you.

What are you capable of that you refuse to acknowledge you are capable of that if you would acknowledge you are capable of it would give you all the possibilities you believe you do not have? Everything that is times a godzillion, will you destroy and uncreate it all? Right and Wrong, Good and Bad, POD and POC, All 9, Shorts, Boys, and Beyonds.

When you commit to your life, you perceive choices and possibilities you never knew could be available. The whole universe changes and everybody you are around changes, too. When you change your point of view and you commit to you and your reality and to creating beyond the limitations of this reality, the universe starts to adjust itself around that. Your commitment to you and your life, to your awareness, and to your reality is the most powerful source of creation on the planet. You are willing to be the leader and go where you are going, whether anybody else goes along or not. You become the invitation for others to go with you, and they have to choose. You do not have to save them anymore.

Committing to your life is being willing to go beyond anything you have decided is *you*.

> *Your commitment to you and your life, to your awareness, and to your reality is the most powerful source of creation on the planet.*

CREATING FROM THE SPACE OF POSSIBILITY

Dain:
Committing to your life is a point that changes all of time. It changes everything that comes after it and lots of things that

came before it. Your world and everything in it changes. You couldn't stop it even if you wanted to.

Before I committed to my life, I got to a place where I realized, "I have been destroying and uncreating limitations for years, but I have never chosen to commit to me and my life." The day after I made the commitment to my life, I could perceive the universe change. Since then, so many of the things I had been asking for and trying to create have started to show up. I recently got an email saying that one of the things I have been trying to create for eight years is going to happen. Really? Damn!

Gary:

When you are committed to your life, people realize you are somebody they want to listen to.

Dain:

People started seeing that I had value and that I could contribute something to them, whereas before they never saw that as a possibility. When I changed, my reality of possibilities was suddenly impinging on theirs in a different way.

Gary:

Once Dain committed to his life, the people around him suddenly started to change and choose something different. They had to choose to be greater because Dain was.

Dain:

When you truly make a commitment to your life, it changes your world *and* other people's worlds. As I acknowledge and allow the commitment, it opens up and allows a different space of being for everyone. I did not realize that before. I had no idea what making a commitment to my life would create. I did not recognize that not committing to my life was a huge missing piece in allowing what I knew should be possible to actually show up.

Committing to your life is so powerful that when you do it, you become part of creating a future where the entire universe can help.

What invention are you using to avoid the commitment to your true life are you choosing? You have created a faux life that you think you are totally committed to. You have a faux life. Would you give up some of your commitment to your faux life? Everything that is times a godzillion, will you destroy and uncreate it, please? Right and Wrong, Good and Bad, POD and POC, All 9, Shorts, Boys, and Beyonds.

Gary:
Look back at a time in your life when everything went boom, boom, boom and fell into place. Was that done from the space of possibility or from the space of conclusion? It was done from the space of possibility. If you create your life from the space of possibility, everything falls into place in a way that knocks your socks off—because nothing is hard.

What are you capable of that if you would acknowledge it would give you all the possibilities you believe you do not have? Everything that is times a godzillion, will you destroy and uncreate it, please? Right and Wrong, Good and Bad, POD and POC, All 9, Shorts, Boys, and Beyonds.

**Committing to your life is so powerful
that you become part of creating a future
where the entire universe can help.**

A LIFE THAT WORKS FOR YOU

Gary:

What if you committed to having a life that works for you whether anybody else likes it or not? What if you said, "I am not living any part of my life according to somebody else's point of view"? That's what it was for me. Whether anybody else agreed with me or liked what I was doing was irrelevant. I was having my life.

At one point years ago, the Internal Revenue Service took all the money I had in the bank for taxes they said I owed. My accountants were telling me I was out of money. So what did I do? I went to Harrods and I bought $31,000 worth of stuff for my antique store in Australia. People asked, "How can you do that when you owe taxes?"

I said, "I owe taxes. I am not dead. And which is a better use of my money? Paying $31,000 to the IRS or buying $31,000 worth of stuff that is worth $90,000?"

Dain:

Most people would stop creating. Gary wouldn't do that.

**What if you committed to having a life that works
for you whether anybody else likes it or not?**

WHAT YOU ARE LOOKING FOR IS NOT OUTSIDE OF YOU

Dain:

You can POD and POC your limitations for years without truly choosing your life. I did that. You can try to commit to something outside of yourself in order to change things. I did that, too. If you commit to something outside of you, when it does not work out—and it never will—you tell yourself you can leave.

Gary:

You say, "Well, I tried to go there, but it did not work out." But here's the thing: What you are looking for is not outside of you. You commit to things outside of you. You are always looking outside of yourself. That is not choosing your life. You have refused to own the gift inside of you. Are you willing to own that you are a gift? No, you aren't. You have not been willing to be that potent. You have never allowed yourself to be the gift you are. You have never been willing to own how powerful and amazing you are.

You have not committed to your life yet because you keep looking for what other people are doing—not what you are doing.

What are you not doing or being that if you choose to do or be it would create a different reality? Everything that is times a godzillion, will you destroy and uncreate it, please? Right and Wrong, Good and Bad, POD and POC, All 9, Shorts, Boys, and Beyonds.

**You have refused to own the gift inside of you.
Are you willing to own that you are a gift?**

ARE YOU COMMITTED TO YOUR PREFERENCES RATHER THAN YOUR LIFE?

Gary:

I was talking with someone who doesn't like to travel. She said, "Sometimes I prefer to be home and not to travel. Is that just a preference? Or does that preclude possibilities?"

I asked, "What do you want to create? If you prefer not to travel, does that limit and eliminate *some* possibilities or a *lot* of them?" You have to ask: 'Is this preference creating a limitation in my life?'"

If you are committed to your preferences, you have not committed to your life. Once you actually make a commitment to your life, you will ask: "How can I create that?" not "How do I get to live the way I prefer to live?"

Oftentimes your preference is a conclusion. You create a difficulty if you are not willing to be aware of what is conclusion and what is preference. If your conclusion is "I would prefer not to eat at McDonalds," that's okay. My conclusion is "I will not eat at cookie cutter restaurants," but if I have no choice but cookie cutter restaurants, do I eat at them? Usually. Actually, I tend to drink instead of eat, because you can get good beer anywhere.

All you have to do is ask: "Is this preference limiting my possibilities?" I preferred living in Santa Barbara, but living there was limiting my possibilities, so I asked: "Where can I go that will create the most possibility?"

Dain:

Gary and I were aware that we needed to function from the space of what would create the greatest future possibilities. We started looking at Houston. Then we found a house and we moved. Once we arrived, I said, "I hate it here!" Sometimes you make a choice based on the awareness of possibilities and if you have a bunch of conclusions, they will show up afterwards. They do not show up beforehand; they show up afterwards, and it's "What the f--k?!"

If you are committed to the possibilities, you get to see all the conclusions that have limited you in the past that are no longer limiting you because you have put yourself in a different situation or a different space, and you get to use the wonderful tools of Access to get over your points of view so you can have the possibilities that you made the change for.

> What have you made so vital about being in absolute op-position and resistance to infinite possibilities that keeps you living in the finite pile of shit that this reality creates as your life? Everything that is times a godzillion, will you de-stroy and uncreate it, please? Right and Wrong, Good and Bad, POD and POC, All 9, Shorts, Boys, and Beyonds.

Gary:

I can live anywhere. I'm interested in what will create the greatest possibility. I once lived in a space the size of a closet for five months. Did I prefer to live in a closet? No. Did I have enough money to not live in a closet? No, but eventually I came out of the closet and chose a lot more. You can live anywhere. You have to ask: "What is going to create the most in my life?" Choose to live what is going to create the most. For us, moving to Houston was going to create the most.

"Is this preference limiting my possibilities?"

WHAT DOES IT MEAN TO LIVE A BIGGER LIFE?

Gary:

I went back to Santa Barbara last weekend and rode my horse. I said, "Oh my God! This place is so beautiful!" Did I miss it? Not at all, because I still have the beauty. The only thing I could miss is the fact that everybody has a life the size of a postage stamp. I'm not interested in that.

Santa Barbara is a stunningly beautiful place and it is so expensive that people are willing to live in a multi-million dollar house the size of one room as though that means they have "arrived." They are special. They say, "We live in the most beautiful place in the world. Of course we're happy." I see the way they're living and I think, "And you would choose this small life in Santa Barbara for what reason?"

Dain:

The small life is having very little reach into the world. Basically you are content with "I live here and it's pretty. This is of value."

Gary:

"And I am valuable because I live here."

Dain:

You get a weird sense of your value because you have a house on the hill. What does that have to do with anything? That is having a small life.

Gary:

When you choose to commit to your life, the things you can choose become more obvious. When you choose to create the life you've committed to, you begin to see "Oh, this choice will lead me where I want to go."

That's why you have to commit to your *life*, not your *preferences*. You cannot truly live if you are not committed to your life.

You have to choose to live and to be in action. We are trying to unlock the place where you have not committed to your life and as a result, you have not yet chosen to actually live. The ongoing action of living will occur once you actually commit to your life and to having your life.

You cannot truly live if you are
not committed to your life.

EASE AND JOY AND GLORY

Gary:

A participant in the Home of Infinite Possibilities class said to me, "I have a lot of ease in my life. I have created a lot of ease, and yet it seems there is something beyond that."

I said, "You are correct. There is a level of ease beyond what you define as ease. It is greater than the ease you have or the ease you know, because you are not yet willing to have all possibilities." People call their life easy when it is not dysfunctional or miserable. They think that if they have less pain in their life, they have ease, or if they do not have to suffer and cope in chaos, they have ease. Possibility is beyond that. And what is it going to take to have possibility? Commitment to your life.

The more you commit to your life, the more the limitations in your life fall away. It's not about fighting to get clear of them and it's not about fighting to get a point of view. It's that the moment you commit to your life, the things that were bothering you disappear. It's all that ease, joy, and glory stuff we talk about: "All of life comes to me with ease and joy and glory."

Dain:

Life becomes easy. It's actually easy.

All of life comes to me with ease and joy and glory.

4
Discovering
There is Choice

Gary:

So as we've been saying, when you make the choice to commit to your life, suddenly all kinds of things start to show up. When you commit, you find out there is choice. Then you choose. You choose and you choose, and every time you choose, different possibilities show up.

Will committing to your life change things? Yes. Could it mean that a relationship ends? Yes. Does that mean it is a bad thing? Maybe not. Maybe it will be the best thing that ever happened to you. It's not bad that something ends.

When something ends, I ask: "What else is possible?" My point of view is that if I lose something, I know I am going to get something better. If I do not get something I want, I will get something better.

Many years ago Dain and I were looking at renting a house in Santa Barbara, but the owners would not commit to us, so we said, "We actually like that other house better even though it is more money. Let's go with that." That was where we needed to be. That is what worked. It got us started on where we are now. Did we lose? No. Did we not commit? No. The owners of the house probably didn't commit to us because we were too much for them in the first place. When people do not commit to you, you may be

39

too much for them to be committed to, so maybe you should look from a different direction.

It also works the other way around. When you are not willing to commit to something, you have decided it is too big a commitment. You do not want to make that kind of commitment. But what if you were willing to look at what you are actually committed to?

> **When people do not commit to you, you may be too much for them to be committed to, so maybe you should look from a different direction.**

"THIS DOES NOT WORK FOR ME"

Gary:

Committing to your life is about knowing what you want. You know where you are going and you know when you are going to go for it. It is not being willing to give *you* up for anybody else.

Dain:

When you commit to your life, you do not make your world about what anybody else is choosing.

Gary:

You are willing to choose what works for you. When something doesn't work for you, use the tool: "This does not work for me." That's all there is to it. "This does not work for me." It's being in allowance. It's different energetically from: "THIS DOES NOT WORK FOR ME!" That's resistance and reaction.

Dain:

When you are resisting anything, you are not committed to your life. You are not committed to your life when you are reacting to anything. You are not committed to your life when you are defending against anything.

> **Committing to your life is about knowing what you want.**

> **You know where you are going and you know when you are going to go for it.**

REVOKING PAST COMMITMENTS

Gary:

Dain and I were talking with a lady who realized she was committed to her mother, but her mother was not committed to her. This lady's sister had committed suicide to avoid being owned by the mother, and the lady's father escaped from his wife by getting Alzheimer's.

Dain:

Those people had checked out, each in their own way, to get away from the woman because that was the only way they thought they could end the commitment. The lady asked, "What can I do different here?"

Gary:

I asked, "Do you have to be committed to your mother?" She said, "No."

I asked, "So, are you willing to revoke all your oaths, vows, swearings, fealties, comealties, and commitments to being with your mother?"

She said, "Wow! Yes."

You can do this with everybody you think you are committed to—even the ones who have died—so you have the freedom to choose something different and so do they.

Will you revoke, recant, rescind, reclaim, renounce, denounce, destroy, and uncreate all your oaths, vows, swearings, fealties, comealties, and commitments for all eternity? Everything that is times a godzillion, will you destroy and uncreate it all? Right and Wrong, Good and Bad, POD and POC, All 9, Shorts, Boys, and Beyonds.

> *Are you willing to revoke all your oaths,*
> *vows, swearings, fealties, comealties,*
> *and commitments for all eternity?*

HAVE YOU MADE A FOREVER COMMITMENT?

Gary:

A friend was having an upset. I asked her, "Who does this belong to? Is this really yours? Is it your father's? Your mother's? Your brother's?" She saw that the upset was her younger brother's. She had made major commitments to him when they were kids and their mother was ill. She used to carry him around. She saw she had committed to carrying him around forever, but she hadn't been aware this commitment existed. As long as she had to carry him on her back, she could not create her life in totality.

She said, "Taking on that responsibility seemed normal to me."

Dain:

She didn't even notice she had taken it on.

Gary:

Why wouldn't she notice it? If that's the way you've been functioning for a long time, it seems normal to you. You make yourself blind to what's controlling you. If you get spanked as a little kid, you think being spanked is normal. The fact that other kids don't get spanked is weird to you.

My friend had committed to *her brother's* life, not *hers.* She was a little kid and she made this commitment, and then many years after the fact, she was trying to make a commitment to her own life—but she couldn't.

She said, "It seems like that upset came up so it could get uncreated and allow me to choose to commit to my life in a different way."

Do you have forever commitments that you have not revoked? All the forever commitments you have from any lifetime that you have not yet revoked, will you revoke, recant, rescind, reclaim, renounce, denounce, destroy, and uncreate them all? Right and Wrong, Good and Bad, POD and POC, All 9, Shorts, Boys, and Beyonds.

**Do you have forever commitments
that you have not revoked?**

COMMITMENT TO A PAST-LIFE RELATIONSHIP

Gary:

I talked with a lady who said, "I've been thinking about your book, *The Place*, and the relationships in it. When I have talked with you about relationships, you have asked me, 'Do you really desire a relationship?' I always say *no*, but I keep going back to the energy I had with a past-life lover, which reminds me of the relationships in *The Place*."

Gary:

I said, "When you have that kind of thing in the past, you tend to make that the ideal scene and you try to create it in the present, but your commitment is to *that* person and *that* relationship, not to creating a relationship in the present that works for you. Being committed to a ghost doesn't work for anyone."

Are you committed to a past-life relationship?

If you are committed to someone from some other lifetime, you can't find this lifetime. You can't have a total commitment to the person you are with this lifetime because you are committed to someone from the past. Will you destroy and uncreate all that? Right and Wrong, Good and Bad, POD and POC, All 9, Shorts, Boys, and Beyonds.

> ***Being committed to a ghost doesn't work for anyone.***

COMMITTING TO YOUR LIFE IS JUST A CHOICE

Gary:

It is just a choice to commit your life and to realize that when you make that commitment, you have no idea where it is going to go. You have no idea what is going to happen. You just know you are going.

Most people want a map. "It's Tuesday," they say. "Are we in Belgium yet?" They want to know that on *this* day, *this* is going to happen because *this* is the place where it is going to happen. But that's not how it works. When you truly commit to your life, your life becomes a constant state of the adventure of creating it.

When you are in an infinite place in that awareness, there is no more control. There is no driving; there is no figuring things out. And there is no motivation. There is no reason for anything; there is just choice.

Most people are not comfortable with having choice. Have you ever gotten a menu that has fifteen pages? How do you decide what to eat? I've learned to close the menu and ask, "Body, what do you want to eat?" then open the menu to whatever page it goes to, and say, "That. Okay, done." That is the way you teach yourself how to be aware of what you want to choose.

You have infinite choice and infinite possibilities, and when you finally commit to your life, the infinite choice and the infinite possibility become very obvious.

Dain:

When you commit to your life, life has a totally different quality to it. You say, "Wow, I did not know living could be this way!"

> **When you truly commit to your life,**
> **your life becomes a constant state of**
> **the adventure of creating it.**

CHOOSE!

If you had no yesterday, what would you create today? Without yesterday, what would today bring you? What would you create? Ask:

- If I was committed to my life what would I choose?
- What possibilities would show up for me that I am not willing to have show up?

You've got ten seconds to choose the rest of your life. What do you want to choose? That is all you need to ask. Can we cut to the chase here? How do you change all this shit right now? You've heard the answer before: "Choose." It's up to you to say, "Okay, I am choosing it now." Once you commit to your life, the commitment is about all the ways in which you can change.

Can we cut to the chase here? How do you change all this shit right now?

You've heard the answer before: "Choose!"

5
Being Owned

Gary:

Dain and I were talking about infinite possibilities with a lady who said, "There are so many businesses I would like to create, that I could create, that I am not creating because I do not want a business to own me."

I asked, "Do you clean your house?" She said, "Yeah, when I have to or when the cleaning lady is sick."

I asked, "So you pay to have your house cleaned?" She said, "Yes."

I said, "If you pay to have your house cleaned, do you own the house? Or does the house own you? The house owns you. The reality is you do not own anything. Everything owns you. If you get that, the idea of being owned does not seem so bad."

Another person said, "The only things I'm cool with owning me are my horse and my dogs. I have not bought a house because I don't want a house to own me."

I said, "There's a difficulty with that. If you are not willing to have anything and everything own you, then you are not willing to own *you* either. You're saying, 'I am not owned by the life I am living. I am not involved in it—because if I am not involved in it, then it does not own me.'"

You give ownership of yourself to all kinds of people, places, and things. You have a car and you love your car. You take good care of it. Do you own it? Or does it own you? It owns you. You love your clothes. You keep them clean and pressed. Do they own you? Or do you own them? They own you. If you realize you are a contribution to something, you don't own it; it owns you.

The reality is you do not own anything. Everything owns you.

If you get that, the idea of being owned does not seem so bad.

DO YOU OWN YOUR BUSINESS? OR DOES YOUR BUSINESS OWN YOU?

Gary:

I was working with a lady who was struggling with her ranch, and at one point it became clear to her that *she* didn't own her ranch; her ranch actually owned *her*. She said, "As soon as I recognized that, the energy of the ranch grew exponentially."

You might think about that if you own a ranch or oil wells or jewelry or anything else. When you recognize that things own you; you can contribute to them in a different way than if you try to own them.

Dain:

Until you commit your life, you can't allow the greatness and the contribution of everything that could own you.

Gary:

There is a greatness in being owned. It means you have capacities. When you're trying to own something, you're trying to eliminate your capacities so you have a way of leaving. That's not being committed to your own life.

> **When you recognize that things own you,**
> **you can contribute to them in a different**
> **way than if you try to own them.**

BEING OWNED BY YOUR BODY

Gary:

You have a body. You may think you own it but you do not love it. You are not nice to it. You do not truly care for it. You are in resistance to it. You kick it around like it is a dog with mange. And then you wonder why it does not do the things you want. The only thing you are actually committed to is your body pain. Why are you committed to pain? Because that is what is real to you. You make that real, whether it is or not.

Your body is committed to you, but you are not committed to it. You will not let it own you, and in so doing, you maintain a separation between you and it at all times. You resist being with it. Do you want to know how to stop doing that? Ask:

- What would I have to do to let my body own me?
- What would that look like?
- What would that be like?

Right now, you own your body because it is willing to do anything for you, but you are not willing to be owned by it, which means there is a constant state of separation between you and it. What can you do to be owned by your body and to own your body?

What energy, space, and consciousness can you be to be totally owned by your body for all eternity? Everything that does not allow that, will you destroy and uncreate it all? Right and Wrong, Good and Bad, POD and POC, All 9, Shorts, Boys, and Beyonds.

When you are willing to be owned by your body, you will not discard it, you will not diss it and make it feel like a piece of shit, nor will you choose pain as your primary source of relationship with it. When you are willing to be owned by your body, you will ask:

- Body, what do you need?
- What do you want?

It's a whole different universe.

Dain:

What would it be like if you were the communion and the joy of being here on this planet? What would it be like if you had the sense of "Oh my God, I get to be *me*! How did I get so lucky?" What if you had that same sense of communion and joy with your body? "How did I get so lucky to have this body? What can I do with this body?" You have to be willing to be owned by your body in order for that to happen.

Gary:

Once you commit to your life, you will allow your body in. When Dain committed to his life, things that had been stuck in his body for a long time started to unlock. If you were willing to be owned by your body, you would have infinite possibilities with it.

"What can you do to be owned by your body and to own your body?"

PEOPLE OWN YOU, TOO

Gary:

People own you, too. My grandson owns me totally. Last night he built a fort in the living room. He said, "Grandpa, you get in here." The fort was so small I had to double-fold myself to get inside. After a while, I said, "Okay, Grandpa has to go to bed now. Grandpa is sleepy. I have to go to sleep."

He said, "You can sleep here." I said, "It is not big enough for me, honey. Thank you for the offer." I weaseled myself out and got away, but he owns me. It is the same with my kids. My kids own me. Why? Because I have made a commitment to them. Whenever you make a commitment to people, they own you.

When my kids were small, I said, "Okay, this child is part of my life." My reality was: "I have a child. I am committed to this." Once some friends called and said, "We are having a Christmas party. We would like you to come, but no children are coming to this party."

I said, "Then neither am I. My kid is part of Christmas for me. My perspective is that Christmas is about children. If you do not want children at your Christmas party, you do not want me, because I do not want to be at Christmas without my kid." Was I willing to give up *me* for my kid? No. Was I willing to acknowledge that I had made a commitment by having a kid? Yes.

Have you spent your life trying to create your independence and prove you are not owned by anyone or anything? When you are trying to prove that you are not owned by anyone or anything, you do not have to make a commitment to your life.

Can you be owned by someone or something without giving up any part of you? The answer is *yes*. I am owned by my grandson *and* I never give up any of me. I am owned by my daughter *and* I never give up any of me. I choose what works for me whether or not it works for them.

51

Being owned by somebody is knowing you will only give up what you choose to give up and you will only be committed to what you choose to be committed to. You are going to do what you want to do because that is what works for you.

What are you refusing to be owned by that you truly could be owned by that if you were owned by it would give you total possibility? Everything that is times a godzillion, will you destroy and uncreate it all? Right and Wrong, Good and Bad, POD and POC, All 9, Shorts, Boys, and Beyonds.

People tell me they find the idea of being owned repellent or distasteful. They have spent their life trying to create their independence.

Dain:
And trying to prove they are not owned by anyone or anything.

Gary:
When you are trying to prove that you are not owned by anyone or anything, you do not have to make a commitment to your life.

Dain:
I did that. I spent my life proving I was not owned by anyone or anything. I thought that was why I chose some of the things I have chosen in my life, like not to get married and not to have kids, but it was not actually that. It was my primary way of not committing to myself and my own life. By the way, I finally did commit.

Gary:

When you are not committed to your own life, can you really commit to someone else's?

What are you refusing to be owned by that you truly could be owned by that if you were owned by it would give you total possibility?

BEING OWNED IS PROVIDING WHAT IS NEEDED—IF IT WORKS FOR YOU

Gary:

I am owned by consciousness because I always choose consciousness over everything else. Consciousness is not a slave driver. Consciousness is a request machine that says, "Here is a possibility. Do you want it? What do you want?"

I will do what will create more consciousness in my grandson's world. Last night my daughter was trying to finish a paper for her class. She needed some time to work on that, and her son was demanding somebody be a slave and pay attention to him. So I became the attention deliverer and she got about half an hour of freedom. That fulfilled what she needed. It was what was required for her and for him. It was not a big deal. It was just a choice.

Being owned is not being subject to others' needs. It's providing what is needed—if it works for you. You have the choice of committing to your family's and other people's needs—or you can see what they require and choose to do what works for you. It's not about taking care of them so you never get to choose otherwise.

Someone I know learned via text that her mother had cancer. She immediately called her parents and said, "Hey, I'm coming to visit this weekend." That was realizing what was required and delivering it. Ease comes from being willing to know what is required—if you choose to do it and to have no resistance. If you choose to do it, you do it.

How do you commit to someone without losing *you* in the process? You recognize that you have let that person own you and you are in the question of possibility. You ask:

- What else is possible here?
- What haven't I considered?
- What could I create beyond this?

Being owned does not take me away from my life because I am committed to my life more than I am committed to being owned by others.

Dain:

You need to do what honors you *and* the commitments you have made to others. When you are in consciousness and you make a commitment to somebody, you honor your commitment *and* you do not destroy you in the process. You need to do both.

Gary:

A friend of ours wanted to go to Venice for a few weeks to do some classes. She chose her reality. She chose for her life. She said, "When I did that, my whole world grew. Doing that showed me how much I have been referencing everything else except my life." At the same time, she knew that being gone that long would tweak her husband, and she was willing to do whatever it took to make it work for him.

Dain:

Committing to your life is doing that every time. And it changes everybody.

Have you been referencing everybody else for everything, including what is possible, what you can choose, how you can get things handled, and especially what is not possible? Everything that is times a godzillion, will you destroy and uncreate it all? Right and Wrong, Good and Bad, POD and POC, All 9, Shorts, Boys, and Beyonds.

Gary:

It is: "I am never going to choose anything but my life, and if there is somebody who does not like it, oh well. If they do like it, oh well. If they think it should be different, oh well."

Do you realize you have been holding yourself back most your life? Do you recognize that you have been on "stop" most of the time? Do you realize there is no red light in front of you? There is a green light. Do you still think it is red? Everything that is times a godzillion, will you destroy and uncreate it all? Right and Wrong, Good and Bad, POD and POC, All 9, Shorts, Boys, and Beyonds.

> *"I am never going to choose anything but my life, and if there is somebody who does not like it, oh well."*

6
No Resistance, No Reaction, No Resentment

Dain:

Gary is totally committed to his own life *and* he is able and willing to contribute to other people more than anybody I have ever met. He does it from no resistance, no reaction, no resentment. He recognizes, "Okay, this is what is required of me right now." You have to get that there are certain things required of you, especially when you are owned by somebody. You do not resist that; you just know it, and it makes your life easier. It's your resistance to people requiring things of you that creates the problem. You go into resistance and you become less present for them. This is the thing that kills most people and their relationships. You resist being owned and in so doing, you cut off the choices and possibilities.

So what can you do? You can say, "Okay, I am owned by this person. Okay, they require this. Okay, I have to deliver this. Okay, fine." And then it is done.

Gary:

It is the resistance and reaction to what is required that makes your life go as slow as it does. I know what is required of me, always. I will deliver what is required because that's what is required, and it is easier not to resist it than it is to avoid it. You slow your life down when you try to avoid things, as though avoidance is going to give you more control or more freedom.

Dain:

Resisting things takes more energy and more time than doing them. Gary functions with such practicality in this area. I am so grateful to see this because I grew up with people who did resistance and reaction to everybody they were committed to and everybody who owned them. I see that in so many relationships. You want somebody to be committed to. You want somebody to own you, and then the moment you get it, you resent it totally. It is as if you're saying, "Darn, I have commitment now. What do I do with it?"

Gary:

I know what I have to do and I just do it. I have no resentment; I have no resistance. I say, "Okay, grandson, I am playing with you." Then I say, "Okay, I am done. I have a life I have to deal with." I know what I have to give, and I will do what is required, and at the same time, I won't be subject to his needs—because that is not functioning from possibility.

You simply realize: "I am committed to this person. This person owns me." Then you ask, "What do I have to do?"

Dain:

Most people, when they are owned, believe they are subject to somebody else's needs. This is a huge part of what creates the resistance, reaction, and resentment to the other person. If you do not make yourself subject to the other person's needs, you can be totally owned and still have total choice and awareness of what is required.

Gary:

You can know what is possible.

Dain:

And not resist and react to anything.

> **You have to get that there are certain things required of you, especially when you are owned by somebody.**
>
> **You do not resist that; you just know it, and it makes your life easier.**

HONORING YOURSELF AND YOUR COMMITMENTS

Gary:

Dain and I were talking with a woman who had been taking care of her mom for seven years. In the process of caring for her mom, the woman got physically exhausted and did not feel she had the option to make the choices she consciously wished to make. She said she felt overrun by an energy that seemed bigger than choice. She was not honoring herself as well as her commitment to her mom.

I asked her, "Is what you're experiencing an awareness of your mother's unwillingness to have choice?" She said, "Yes!" This is something many of us do. We believe other people's unwillingness somehow has a relationship to us. What do you do in that situation?

Dain:

You need to do what honors you *and* the commitments you have made to others.

What have you made so vital about defending your contribution or your lack thereof that keeps you from creating the reality of infinite possibilities you truly be that you do not want to know that you be that if you would actually choose to be that which you know you be would make everything ease, joy, and glory in totality with total ease for all eternity? Will you destroy and uncreate it please? Right and Wrong, Good and Bad, POD and POC, All 9, Shorts, Boys, and Beyonds.

> **You need to do what honors you and the commitments you have made to others.**

BEING THE LEADER OF YOUR OWN REALITY

Gary:

A class participant asked, "What would committing to my life look like in regard to choosing beyond the confines of my nuclear family?"

I said, "For me it is recognizing that the nuclear family is great and appropriately named."

Dain:

It is like an atom bomb waiting for a moment to go off.

Gary:

You have to be willing to be the leader of your own reality and go where you are going to go, no matter what. You can have a nuclear family and still be the leader of your own reality. You can go where you need to go and not limit you based on making your family the be-all and the end-all.

Dain:

So you are owned, but you never have to give up you, which is weird because it does not make any sense.

Gary:

It does not make sense because in this reality, commitment means you promise to give up everything for the other person. That's not what we're talking about. Committing to your life is saying, "Whatever it takes, I am going to have a life that works for me." When you know you are owned by somebody, you do not resist them. Resistance is not a possibility.

> **You have to be willing to be the leader**
> **of your own reality and go where you**
> **are going to go, no matter what.**

WHAT DOES RESISTANCE DO?

Gary:

A class participant said, "For the last four days, I have been working with my dad. Never before have I been with my dad for four days without getting annoyed or irritated. There is so much space. Does this have to do with the willingness to be owned?"

I said, "When you recognize, 'I can be owned by my dad,' he no longer has control over you. When you can be owned by your mother and your brother, they will no longer have control over you. Being owned doesn't mean you're going to do what they want. You're not their slave. But if you resist being a slave, then you are a slave to resistance, which means you have to fight everything."

When you commit to your life, you do what is required to create it—and you don't resist any of it. If I know I have to make a phone call, I make a phone call. If I am out to dinner and five people text me, I will text them back while carrying on a conversation with my dinner mates. I know it is rude, but I am not willing to wait until later to deal with something.

Dain:

Gary does not wait on anything. He would rather call someone back now and get it over with. This is part of the way he creates. Most people leave so many things undone that their rivers dam up and there is no creative flow. There is only a little trickle of water because of the backlog of things they have not done. All of their energy is going back to the things that are undone. They're like giant boulders blocking the creative flow.

Gary:

The energy of taking care of something comes in and people say, "I'm going to put that on my list." And then when they go back to their list, the energy to do it is no longer there, so they never do it. They're putting off what will create their life.

If you are resisting calling somebody back, you have given them ownership over you, and your resistance equals ownership.

Dain:

Gary is not a slave to anyone or anything. Even when he is owned, he is not a slave because he is not doing resistance and reaction to the ownership. He is aware of the ownership because he is not subject to people's needs.

Gary:

A *need* is anything someone thinks is important to them. I am not subject to people's needs. I will provide their needs if it suits me.

I have people who "need" me to talk to them for hours on end about nothing at all. So I talk to them. Do I do it for hours? No, I give them ten minutes then I say, "You know what? I am really sorry but I have to go. That is all I can do now. You want to call me later? Sure."

I have sucked enough energy out of their universe or I have provided so much energy to them that they don't need to call me back. The best way to get people out of their need and greed, their need to have and hold onto, is to flow energy to them when you talk to them. Suddenly they do not need to talk anymore.

When you commit to your life, you do what is required to create it— and you don't resist any of it.

7
Playing the Game of Infinite Possibilities

Gary:

If you really want to create the game of life, you might want to learn how to play chess. On this planet, chess is the closest thing to a game that is played from possibilities. If you are willing to win the game, it becomes a game of living—a game of infinite possibilities. You look at every move you make and how that could create the next five to seven moves for the other person, and how each one of those moves would create five to seven moves for you and your board. If you anticipate all the other person's moves and all the places they are going to go, who is going to be the winner of the game? You!

When you're a great chess player, everybody in the world is a pawn in your reality. And if you learn to play both sides of the board, you can try to outmaneuver yourself, which expands every aspect of your life and living because you are always looking at every other possibility, no matter what is going on.

For me, that is the joy of living. "Okay, he made that move. Now what?" Because I have no point of view, I can take any point of view, and as a result, I have available all the moves that are available in the game of living—all the moves that can create a different possibility at all times.

> *Because I have no point of view, I can take any point of view, and as a result, I have available all the moves that are available in the game of living.*

EVERY CHANGE IS ANOTHER SET OF POSSIBILITIES

When you live from "Every change is another set of possibilities," change is never a wrongness or badness. Most of us were taught that change is a terrible thing, so we try not to change anything except our underwear.

You are more interested in your plans and your purposes and the necessity of getting it right than you are in the game of playing around to see what else is possible. You don't realize that every choice creates a change and every choice creates a new set of possibilities.

Every time you turn a corner, something new shows up. Recently Dain and I were on our way to lunch when we saw a giant sign that said "Estate Sale." My justification for stopping at the sale was that we needed some beds to stage a house we were selling. I thought, "Maybe I'll find a bed here," because estate sales usually sell beds really cheap. Did I want to put expensive beds in this house? No. I just wanted to get something that would allow people to look at a room and say, "Oh, I could put a bed there," because in general, people are not very imaginative. I used to sell houses. I know this.

Clients would say they wanted a fixer-upper, so I would take them to see a house that was a fixer. They'd say, "No, no, no. I don't want anything this bad," so I'd take them to a house that needed new carpeting. They'd say, "Oh yeah, this is right up my alley." I learned that people can't imagine things. They can't see how things can be changed. I'd ask, "What if you changed that?" and they would say, "What?!" For me changing something is easy. For them it was unimaginable.

So Dain and I stopped at the sale to see if we could find a bed to put into the house we were selling. There were no beds, and all the furniture they had was modern, which is something I don't choose to live with. However, because I'm always aware of possibilities, I noticed a brand new, absolutely stunning white leather couch. I didn't even have to sit in it to know it was comfortable. I remembered that a friend had been looking for a new couch to put in her modern house, so I called her and said, "Hey, come to this place. There's a couch here. Check it out." She came right over. The couch was in perfect condition. They were asking $6,000 for it, and she got it for $1,500.

The possibilities of what my friend was looking for were in my awareness, and the possibility of awareness opens the door for the possibility of achieving what everybody desires. That's the way that possibilities open up. When you look for the infinite possibilities, all kinds of strange things show up.

> *Every choice creates a change and every*
> *choice creates a new set of possibilities.*

WHAT IF THERE WAS NOTHING TO OVERCOME?

Gary:

In this reality, people think you are supposed have challenges to overcome so you can prove that you are powerful enough to overcome a challenge. But what if there was nothing to overcome?

People do not have the point of view that possibility is real—but they do have the idea that if something is impossible, they have to overcome it to prove that anything is possible. It's cuckoo. They think that overcoming the impossible proves they are powerful. But why do they have to prove that overcoming the impossible equals power when they could choose the possibility that creates power?

When you are willing to function from infinite possibility, you are so powerful that nobody can stop you. Why would you try to overcome what you have decided is impossible in order to prove you are powerful enough to overcome the impossible? You would work that hard for what reason?

What choice are you not willing to be? The choice you are not willing to be is all possibilities. If everything was possible in life, what could you not have? Limitation is the only thing you could not have.

Dain:

What invention are you using to avoid the commitment to your true life you could truly be choosing? Everything that is times a godzillion, will you destroy and uncreate it, please? Right and Wrong, Good and Bad, POD and POC, All 9, Shorts, Boys, and Beyonds.

> **When you are willing to function
> from infinite possibility, you are so
> powerful that nobody can stop you.**

CREATION FROM THE SPACE OF INFINITE POSSIBILITIES

Gary:

At the end of the Home of Infinite Possibilities class, someone said, "This is the first time I perceive the space in my head where there are no thoughts, no emotions, and no feelings. There is just space."

I said, "Now we are getting someplace!" I'm mentioning this because sometimes people perceive the space in their head and think, "Oh, I am blank." No, you are not blank; you are space. You cannot help but receive.

Creation from the space of infinite possibilities is where you have no thoughts—but you have massive amounts of awareness and you receive everything with no point of view.

Dain:

The key here is *with no point of view*. We have points of view about everything we perceive. But when we receive with no point of view, it is all cool.

Do you realize that what you call your mind is actually your awareness of everybody else's fixed points of view in this reality?

Gary:

Your mind is dangerous thing because it is not yours in the first place.

Dain:

When you are looking without a point of view, you can perceive the energy of what will be created by a choice.

Gary:

I told a friend that she needed to spend Christmas with her family because if she didn't, she was going to lose her inheritance. I could see what would be created by her choice. She said, "But I do not want to do that."

I said, "Okay, if you are fine about losing your inheritance, no problem."

She asked, "What do you mean that I'll I lose my inheritance? They won't do that."

I said, "Yes, they will. Is your family judging you? If they are judging you, they are going to look for an excuse not to give you anything. It is just the way it is. It does not mean anything."

> **When you are looking without a point of view, you can perceive the energy of what will be created by a choice.**

NO POINT OF VIEW INVITES POSSIBILITY

Gary:

I am always looking for the possibility. I'm always asking:

- What is possible that I have not yet considered?
- What is available that has not been chosen?

Dain:

Gary lives as the space of possibilities. When you are that space, when you do not have a point of view, things come to you. They just keep coming.

Gary:

And when you have a point of view, you push everything away.

"No point of view" invites possibility. That is the reason I keep trying to get you to use "Interesting point of view that I have this point of view" for every point of view you have, for at least six months. "Interesting point of view" reminds you that whatever the judgment is, it's just a point of view that you or someone else has at that moment in time. It is not right or wrong or good or bad. It is just a point of view. When you can do that, you allow things to be what they are. Most people will do this for six minutes and then they'll say, "Oh, this is so much work!" But here's the thing: When you do "Interesting point of view," you own the judgment; it doesn't own you. And when you own judgment, you invite possibility.

> **"Interesting point of view" reminds you that whatever the judgment is, it's just a point of view.**
>
> **When you do "Interesting point of view," you own the judgment; it doesn't own you.**

OWNING JUDGMENT

Gary:

Owning judgment is realizing where you judge. You need to own that you have judgment just like everyone else. When you're truly in allowance of the judgment, you own it. When you resist and react to the judgment, you are aligning and agreeing with it, and the judgment owns you.

Dain:

When you become aware of a space of kindness where before there was judgment or hatred, you see that judgment and hatred do not have to exist. And when you see that it does not have to be that way, you can POD and POC everything that does not allow kindness to come into the world. All of a sudden the space for kindness opens up for everyone who is willing to have it. Everybody who has ever come to Access, whether or not they know it, can step into a space of being that has never been available before.

Gary:

Ask yourself: "Am I *owned by* this judgment or do I *own* this judgment?" Owning the judgment is total allowance. Being owned by the judgment is aligning and agreeing and resisting and reacting to it. And the thing is: Judgment is just judgment; it doesn't mean f--k all.

Owning judgment is realizing where you judge.

WHAT MIGHT BE POSSIBLE IF YOU DID NOT HAVE ANY JUDGMENT?

Gary:

Dain and I were talking with a teacher who had been working at a school for three years. She said, "I know I am a major contribution to the kids I teach, but at the same time, I feel done with this job. Am I being selfish for desiring to create a reality that does not include teaching in this way? And would choosing what seems selfish actually do more for me?"

I said, "It's not complicated. When you are done with a job, you are done with a job. It does not mean you are doing anything bad or wrong by leaving. What might be possible if you did not have any judgment?"

Dain:

I said, "It's possible that your complicated series of judgments will not allow you to perceive what is actually available for you to choose and be."

Gary:

In order to commit to your life, you have to be clueless, which means you have no judgment and no fixed points of view. There is nothing you can rely on except the fact that you are committed to your life and you are going to follow whatever possibilities present themselves. That's just the way it is.

When you are not thinking and judging, you have the ability to create. When you are thinking, you have stepped away from creation and into limitation. That is a brilliant thing I just said. When your brain is fried, you are actually ready for creation. Everything that is times a godzillion, will you destroy and uncreate it all? Right and Wrong, Good and Bad, POD and POC, All 9, Shorts, Boys, and Beyonds.

**When you are not thinking and judging,
you have the ability to create.**

**When you are thinking, you have stepped
away from creation and into limitation.**

8
Making More of You Available for Sex, Relationship, Marriage, and Partnership

Gary:

Once you commit to your life, more of *you* is available for you as well as everybody else in your life.

Dain:

Most people try to have a marriage or a partnership without committing to their life, which means they can't commit to anything other than a tiny portion of the entire universe to somebody else. And then they wonder why the marriage or partnership does not work. How could a marriage or partnership possibly work if you are not making a choice to be everything that is possible with somebody? If you are only willing to be a tiny portion of that, that is all you are willing to have of *you*.

> **How could a marriage or partnership possibly work if you are not making a choice to be everything that is possible with somebody?**

THE PERFECT RELATIONSHIP OF YOU WITHOUT YOU

Gary:

You never learn to know *you*, value *you*, look at *you*, or actually examine *you*—and then you ask, "What is really true for me?" As long as you do not know what is true for you, you do not have to choose who you are, so you can be whatever you want. You end up being a chameleon who seems to fit in everywhere without ever fitting in anywhere, especially not in your own life. That is how you create the pretense of not being. You think, "Someday someone will see me."

Dain:

"Someday somebody will find me." But every time someone gets close to you, you shut them down faster than anything you've ever done. You find a way to judge them. You find a way to say they're doing something wrong. You say, "I can't believe you did that thing to me three months ago."

Gary:

As long as you don't have to see *you*, they can't see you. As long as they can't see you, you don't have to see *you*. And as long as that occurs, you don't have to actually have a life. You have the perfect relationship of you without *you*.

You work hard to make yourself into nothing. You work hard to prove that you are not enough, that you are never enough, and that you could never be enough, and even if you were enough, you wouldn't be *you*, so therefore you're not enough.

Dain:

Most relationships are a way of continuously spinning around and around without ever actually moving forward. You're trying to prove that you're getting this reality right, and at the same time you're trying to prove that you have value and you're not a loser.

> *You never learn to know you, value you, look*
> *at you, or actually examine you, and then*
> *you ask, "What is really true for me?"*

NO ONE CAN RECEIVE YOU UNTIL YOU COMMIT TO YOURSELF

Gary:

Are you willing to look at what is really true for you? Here's the thing: No one can receive you until you commit to yourself.

What do you have to be or do different to commit to your life? Choose. It is the one answer I give all the time and everybody says, "I hate it when you say that it is just a choice."

Every place where you've decided you will not look at what is true for you because if you actually had to look at what is true for you, you'd have to look at you, which would mean you would have to know what you really want to choose, which would mean you would need to have the sense that you had some kind of value, whether anybody else thought you were valuable or not. As long as you don't do that, you don't have to actually choose for you and you don't have to choose your life. And you get to make sure that everybody else is wrong and you're right, somehow.... Everything that is times a godzillion, will you destroy and uncreate it all? Right and Wrong, Good and Bad, POD and POC, All 9, Shorts, Boys, and Beyonds.

*Are you willing to look at what
is really true for you?*

WHAT IF YOU ACKNOWLEDGED THE MAGNANIMOUS BEING YOU ARE?

Gary:

Someone we were talking with said, "I have an awareness of what ought to be possible between people, and because of that, I notice that I make a lot of insane choices when it comes to sex and relationship. I find myself in situations where people can't receive me or what I am offering. It feels like I am trying to make the best out of what is available even though I know something greater ought to be possible."

Do you find yourself in situations like this? People cannot receive you because they cannot receive what they cannot be.

Dain:

You are expecting somebody to receive a truly magnanimous being called you.

Gary:

You have never acknowledged that, have you? What if you acknowledged the magnanimous being you are? What if you looked at the other person and asked: "Can this person be what I want them to receive?"

It is simple, but we make it complex. We say, "But I love them. They are so cute and sexy."

Dain:

We say, "I see what they could be if they would just choose to be it."

Gary:

Do you always choose fixer-uppers who you just *know* will eventually realize they are loved because you love them so much? Have you noticed that doesn't work out very well? People who cannot receive love cannot be love.

People cannot receive what they cannot be. You try to give them love because you want them to know that they are loved. I know because I did it—twice. I thought that my commitment to marriage would get my ex-wives to realize I truly loved them. Did they ever receive love? No. Can they love? No.

Dain:

People who cannot receive love cannot be love. If someone is not willing to be something, they cannot receive it. The question to ponder is: "Is this person willing to be what I am trying to give them?"

Gary:

Ask that when you start thinking, "Oh, this person could be a relationship for me."

Dain:

I have seen some of the most phenomenal people, angels who don't realize they have sprouted wings, and they're saying, "If that person would just, just, just, just, just..."

Gary:

If there is a *just* in it, do not go there.

> **What if you looked at the other person and asked:**
> **"Can this person be what I want them to receive?"**

TRUE OWNERSHIP IS THE WILLINGNESS TO BE RECEIVED UTTERLY

Gary:

In a phenomenal relationship, people are willing to receive each other. They are willing to own each other *and* they never give up themselves in order to make the other person happy.

You may think you only have the choice of committing to another person's needs or taking care of them. When you do that, you never get to choose otherwise. What you can do is see what they need and then choose what works for you.

True ownership is the willingness to be received utterly and totally. When you are willing to be received totally, you can allow somebody to own you. And they can only own the part of you that they are willing to receive.

You keep trying to find somebody who will see all of you. Good luck with that. Most people will only own the parts of you they have defined as something they are willing to receive. But if you are willing to be received in totality, you own them, and you are willing to be owned to whatever degree they are willing to receive.

When you are willing to be owned, you have the willingness to be everything and to recognize what people can receive. You have to be willing to be everything. You have to be willing to recognize what people can receive and to know the degree to which they are willing to receive.

Dain:

No one can receive you until you commit to yourself. That's part of the blame game and spinning around in relationships. You get mad at people for not receiving you.

Gary:

You ask, "How can you not get who I truly am? Don't you see how much I love and care for you?" We wouldn't have any traumas and dramas on TV without those lines.

Dain:

We would not have any traumas and dramas in relationship if people were actually committed to their own lives. Trauma and drama wouldn't exist.

Gary:

Commit to your own life and then all of a sudden everything starts to work—even relationships!

True ownership is the willingness to be received utterly and totally.

When you are willing to be received totally, you can allow somebody to own you.

9

What are the Infinite Possibilities with Kids?

Gary:

My three-year-old grandson Zander is an example of an intact being. His mother does not require him to be someone other than who he is.

Dain:

She does not require him to be someone who fits into this reality. When he is cranky, she asks, "Dude, what is going on? How are you doing? What can I do for you? You can choose this as long as you want, but is there anything I can do for you?"

He'll say, "No."

She'll say, "Well, then, have fun." She does not try to get him to fit into this limited reality. She does not try to get him to do what is "right." She does not try to make him wrong. She does not tell that anything he has chosen is wrong, ever. She'll just say, "Dude, this is a choice. When you do this, it frustrates me and it frustrates Grandpa. Are you sure you want to do that?"

He'll say, "I do not want to frustrate Grandpa," and she'll say, "Okay, then, choose something else."

> **"Dude, this is a choice. When you do this, it frustrates me and it frustrates Grandpa. Are you sure you want to do that?"**

CHOICE

Dain:

Look at this for just a moment: "This frustrates me, and it frustrates Grandpa."

"I do not want to frustrate Grandpa."

"Well, then, choose something else."

Zander's mom is giving him choice: the awareness that he can choose something else. He may or may not choose it. This reality weighs on everybody to the best of its ability, but he has that space so he is not fragmented into this reality and out of his reality. From his point of view, the world is his reality.

You are being a cranky bitch or cranky bastard. What is the value of that? Choose something else. We do not realize, right there, that we can go to something else. It is being willing to go to: "I have all kinds of stuff that is pushing on me, but I'm not going to let that determine my reality. I am going to be as happy or as kind and gentle as I want to be."

The question is: "What choice do I have here that I am not choosing?"

Gary:

Zander's mom has also made it quite apparent to him that he has slaves. From his point of view, of course, that is how it is supposed to be. She has shown him how to ask nicely, so he walks up to me and he asks, "Grandpa, would you play with me?" Try to turn that down!

Dain:

If you look at what he's doing from this reality, you could say, "That child should be taught x, y, z. He shouldn't have all those people playing with him and doing things for him." But is that really true? There is no unkindness in his world.

I know for a fact that if my family, who taught me to judge what was appropriate and what was not, were to look at that, they would say, "Well, it's inappropriate for a child to have somebody he can ask something of who would actually do it for him."

Why is that inappropriate? Shouldn't we all have had that? Shouldn't we all have had somebody who was willing play with us and do whatever we wanted? The other night I was playing with Zander for a while. I was tired and I said, "I'm sorry, Zander, I am too tired to play. I need to go to sleep. I need to wake up early tomorrow. I am going to go to bed. I love you."

He said, "Okay." I kissed him on the head and went to bed.

Most of us were not given choice. We had to fight for choice, and we tend to think that if we had been given choice, we would have become stupid, out-of-control people who destroyed the world. No. If we had been given choice as kids, we would have recognized that we can choose anything. We would have become people who contributed to the world and chose what would create more for everybody.

Gary:

A lady we know had been bringing her son to Access classes since he was five. One day the boy came home from being with his dad and said, "Mom, being with you is the difference between being with love and being with hate. Please do not make me go to Dad's again."

She called me and asked, "Oh my God! What do I do?"

I said, "Do not ever make him go there," and she never did.

If we had been given choice as kids, we would have recognized that we can choose anything.

We would have become people who contributed to the world and chose what would create more for everybody.

REQUEST

Gary:

One day my daughter took Zander to the park. He was letting his cars run down the slide. A little kid came over and grabbed his car. Zander said, "Can I have my car back, please?"

The kid said, "No."

Zander looked at him and asked, "Want to play?"

The kid said, "Sure."

So Zander and the kid were playing. The kid let the car fall into the sand and Zander said, "Can you clean that up, please?" He does not like sand on his things or on his body. The kid brushed the sand off the car.

Zander played with this kid and asked him to do things and the kid started doing what Zander asked. Zander has learned that requests will be made of him and that when he follows a request everything gets easier. He has learned that requesting things is the way to get what you want in life. To request it. Were you allowed to have choice when you were a kid? No, you had to do things. You were given one choice: your parents' and teachers' way or the highway.

Dain:

If you request something, the universe will do its best to rearrange itself to make that show up, but few of us request from awareness. We make requests from unawareness, conclusions, judgments, and points of view. The thing you request could come to you with great ease, but it does not have a chance to do so because it is overwhelmed by the requests you are making from stupidity.

Gary:

With my grandson, request is: "Can you please stop that?"

He will say, "Waaah," and I'll ask, "Can you please stop that? It is really annoying."

He will say, "Oh, okay," and stop.

When I ask him to do something, if I explain to him why I want him to do it, he will do it. He is not stupid; he is just uneducated about what is being asked of him.

Dain:

As Zander got closer to being three years old, things started changing in his world; for example, he would not take naps in the afternoon and he would not go to sleep at night. One day when we were having lunch at a restaurant, he was being a little asshole to his mom. He was yelling and trying to hit her. He walked away and went around the corner as if to say, "I am leaving now," which is so frigging cute for someone who is almost three. His mom asked Gary, "Grandpa, are you going to talk to him?"

I said, "I will go talk to him," so I walked around the corner. He was checking to see if anyone was following him because when you're three, you don't really want to be left alone. You act like you do, but you don't, just like most of us now, who are still three.

I grabbed his hand and walked with him. I said, "We need to have a talk." He said, "Okay." I was looking for a booth where we could sit, but none were available so we sat on the doormat at the entrance to the restaurant. I said, "Look, my friend, I realize how difficult this can be, as your world is changing. You are coming into new awarenesses and new possibilities and you do not know what the heck is going on. I understand that. The thing is, hitting people and yelling at them is not going to work. It is not only inappropriate; it is also not the kindness of you. It is not the kindness you want to be in the world."

He was just listening. I said, "I will always be here for you and I will have your back. If you ever need anything, ask for me. Call on me energetically or call on me physically. If you need me, I will be there. You are not alone in this transition. I realize how tough it can be. You are probably going to go through thousands of these transitions by the time you are my age. I will be there for you in any way I can, so we can do this a little more kindly and gently for you."

He just sat there. For a while, we looked out at the sun and the sky glinting off the buildings then he gave me a hug and we walked back to the table. What else would be possible if we did not act from everything we have been handed by this reality and instead went with our knowing?

Gary:

Instead of trying to control kids, what if we acknowledged what was going on in their world? The only reason they are acting out is because they do not understand what is happening.

> **What else would be possible if we did not act from everything we have been handed by this reality and instead went with our knowing?**

THE LANGUAGE OF ENERGY

Dain:

A little kid named Mason used to come to Access classes with his mom. When he first showed up, he was a cool little guy. Then at some point, he suddenly turned into an asshole. He became a prankster. He was doing things to undermine people. I pulled him aside and said, "Dude, I totally get the necessity of doing that. I get the way that it feels. I get the energy you are perceiving and how it swirls around you. I get how you want to make some sense of it and how if you do what you're doing, it feels like you can dissipate it for a while—but is that actually the kindness of you? What do you want to choose in the world?"

I was willing for him to choose to be an asshole. It was just: "I want you to know I am here for you and I understand. Choose what you need to, but if you ever require my contribution, just ask." He did not say anything. He was totally silent.

A few months after that conversation, Mason was at a stable where autistic kids go to ride horses. Gary and I have talked in our classes about how autistic people want to communicate psychically. Well, Mason saw an autistic kid on a horse, and without using any words, he said, "Hi. My name is Mason. Nice to meet you."

The kid, who was six years old and had never spoken before, said, "Mason, Mason." Mason had communicated with the kid in a way the kid could receive, using the language of energy. His parents were completely blown away by what had happened.

The difficulty for kids, especially autistic kids, is that what they communicate is often never received. This is especially difficult when we are young. We "think" something at our parents and implore them to give us something or to do something for us, but the communication is not received because the parents have long ago given up the language of energy because *their* parents would not receive it. Everyone decides that kind of communication cannot exist. By the time you came along, the ability to communicate in this way was long gone to them. You know how people talk about lost languages? The language of energy is one of those lost languages, but it should not have to be lost anymore.

Gary:

It is not lost; it is just no longer "spoken."

Dain:

It has been buried due to this reality's ability to bury it.

A lot of the parents of the children we work with choose something different. They break that pattern so their kids do not have to go through what the parents went through when *they* were kids. If parents do the work that is required to get rid of their limitations, it is a lot easier for kids to let theirs go.

Gary:

It's a choice we make.

> *If parents do the work that is required*
> *to get rid of their limitations, it is a*
> *lot easier for kids to let theirs go.*

BECOMING A CATALYST FOR CHANGE IN THE WORLD

Dain:

Once at an Access class that was attended by adults and kids, a little guy was watching me work with people on a massage table. He jumped on a nearby table that nobody was on and said, "I am ready for a session."

I said, "Okay. What is your name?"

He said, "Joey."

"How old are you?"

"Eleven."

I asked him, "If you could have anything you wanted out of this session, what would it be?"

"I don't want to be a bad person anymore."

I said, "Tell me what you are talking about. What do you mean?"

Joey told me, "When I was a little kid, I would do anything my mom asked. I was really nice to her. Then one time my cousins were staying with us, and they told me I was a stupid mama's boy. They made me wrong for being nice to my mom. I said, 'I am never going to be that way again and ever since then I have been a bad person.'"

I said, "Wow, okay," and I started to work on him. At one point while he was face down on the table, I had my hand on his back and he just relaxed. I felt my hand sink into his back and into his world and into his reality. I thought, "Wow, this kid is here in a way he has never been before." I flipped him over and worked on him some more and then got him up. He looked happy and alert.

I thought, "This is awesome." He went off and came back with his arms full of bottles of water. He asked, "Are you thirsty?" I said, "Thank you!" I saw him later when we were having lunch and he looked happy to be alive, probably for the first time in ages.

Later in the day, I worked on the principal of his school. I said, "I had Joey on the table a while back, and this is what he asked for."

She said, "I have known that boy since he was about five years old. Something happened in his world and from that point forward, he has been the band leader for everything mean that has happened in our school. He has been behind other kids beating people up and stealing their stuff. He has been in charge of everything that has been hurtful to other kids. You can trace almost all of the bad things that have happened in the school back to him."

I said, "Really? Well, that is what he asked for, and I felt it change."

She said, "If you have changed this, it will be a gift to humanity."

A few months later, Gary asked a friend of ours who lives in the city where that school is, to take something to the principal.

Our friend and the principal started talking about the kids and the principal mentioned how much Joey had changed. She said that the kids who were at that Access class with us, including Joey, had become the leaders in the school. They were showing everybody there is a different possibility available, and that hatred, meanness, and unkindness do not have to occur.

This is the kind of change we would like to see in the world, where judgment, vilification, and abuse no longer exist, and a different world is possible. This is what infinite possibilities are about.

When you choose to function from infinite possibility, this becomes who you are in the world. You create a different possibility with every person you talk to. What if you knew that you, being you, would create those kinds of changes in the world? It is a choice. That is all it is. It's a choice you get to make. You just have to choose it.

If what is at the heart of what you desire to create and bring to the world is kindness and possibilities, you will create that. Stop believing it cannot exist. Stop believing this reality is more powerful than what is possible.

Gary:

You have possibilities—but you have to choose them.

Dain:

Fewer people than you think can shift the balance of how the universe spins. Are you willing to be one of those people who does that?

Gary:

Everything you have done to refuse to be the catalyst of change you truly be, will you destroy and uncreate all that?

Right and Wrong, Good and Bad, POD POC, All 9, Shorts, Boys, and Beyonds.

When you choose to function from infinite possibility, this becomes who you are in the world.

10

Creation and the Space of Possibility

Gary:

People often struggle with the idea of creating outside this reality. They say, "If I want to create *outside* this reality then it's impossible to create *in* this reality." That's a lie. You have to look at this reality and ask: "How can I use this reality to my advantage?" You have to use this reality to create outside this reality.

Instead of doing that, you try to fit in, you try to get it right, and you try to look at what's normal. You don't ask, "How can I use this to my advantage?" How come? Have you decided it's wrong to take advantage?

If you are committed to your life, you know exactly what you can manipulate into existence so you get what you want. Are you any good at manipulating to get things you want? Or are you brilliant at it? You're terribly brilliant, but you do not want to acknowledge you are brilliant at it, do you?

It's hard for you to acknowledge your brilliance. You say brilliant things but you never call them brilliant because that would be bragging. You might say, "Boy! That was frigging brilliant. Did I do that great or what?" to yourself, but you won't say it to anybody else.

I don't share my brilliance with everybody else, either, not because I don't want to brag, but because if they are not smart enough to know that I'm brilliant, I can take advantage of them better.

Dain:

Have you never even thought about what *take advantage* means? What the hell is that? You're not willing to have life be that easy. And if you were, would it be the change that this reality requires?

Gary:

There is only one thing you want hard in life. Everything else should be easy.

You have to use this reality to create outside this reality.

You have to look at this reality and ask: "How can I use this reality to my advantage?"

STEALING OTHER PEOPLE'S TALENTS

Gary:

I was talking with friend who said she would like to have some of the talents our brilliant attorney has. She said, "Our attorney has an instinct for going right to the heart of an issue. Is that something that you're born with or is that something that you can learn?"

I said, "If you don't have that talent, watch somebody who has it and say, 'I want that. I'd like to steal that talent.'" You have to be willing to steal other people's talents. This doesn't mean they're going to lose that talent or they are going to have less. It means you're going to have it too. You have to be willing to steal it because you can't collect it by osmosis.

When I steal our attorney's ability to deal with financial stuff, do I end up with less or more? More! And she ends up with more as I steal it.

You won't steal from others because you don't want to leave them without anything, but that's not how it works. When you take something like that from somebody and you become part of it, you acknowledge their ability, which increases it. You put your energy into seeing the value of it, which means they get to see more of the value of what they're capable of. And in the process, they become more, you become more, and the whole world becomes more.

Are you having a hard time receiving this? It's because you decided that stealing is bad or you were taught that stealing is bad. You were taught that stealing is bad by people who stole. They stole your soul with that point of view. And then you got to live in judgment of you for even vaguely considering that you might steal something.

What did they steal from you? Your very soul. Your willingness to commit to your own life. Everything that is times a godzillion, will you destroy and uncreate it all? Right and Wrong, Good and Bad, POD and POC, All 9, Shorts, Boys, and Beyonds.

You have to be willing to steal
other people's talents.

This doesn't mean they're going to lose that
talent or they are going to have less.

It means you're going to have it too.

CHANGE AND NO CHANGE

Gary:

Many people think that change of any kind is destructive. Does that give them more choice or less choice? Less or none. They do not want a high level of choice or change because they cannot control it. They think that no change means things will stay the same. But nothing ever stays the same. Everything always changes. You have to be willing to recognize change when it occurs and go on from there. Will that make your life easier? Yes.

Someone told me she expects change all the time. She never assumes people will do what they say, so she asks them, "Are we still doing this?"

I said, "No, that is not what you ask. Wait and see what people do and then you will know, 'Oh. This is what they meant.' You are trying to guarantee that they are going to make a change they said they would make—but they aren't going to tell you the truth. You have to watch and see what they actually choose. People say all kinds of things to me, and I say, 'Okay.' Then I wait to see what they do. Learn a new strength. It is called patience. Be aware. Wait and see."

What forms of lack of change have you adopted from others that keep you from being aware of the infinite possibilities you can choose and create? Everything that is times a godzillion, will you destroy and uncreate it all? Right and Wrong, Good and Bad, POD and POC, All 9, Shorts, Boys, and Beyonds.

You have to be willing to recognize change when it occurs and go on from there.

TORTURING AND BEING TORTURED

Gary:

Instead of recognizing change, we tend to choose something and stay with it forever. I knew somebody who had been employed by a company for twenty years. He talked all the time about how much he hated his job.

One day I asked him, "If you hate your job so much, why don't you change something? Why don't you leave?"

He said, "I can't leave. The pay and the benefits are too good."

I said, "Torturing yourself by doing something you don't like—what benefit is that? Like the job or get out of the job. Don't sit there and say, 'It is torture and I hate it,' while you're staying for a benefit and not looking at the torture and how that benefits you!"

Where has constantly being tortured been a benefit to you? It is called having a family. It is called having money problems. It is called believing in your culture. It is called, "I belong." It is called, "I do not belong." It has millions of names and it is all of the ways in which you torture yourself. Everything that is times a godzillion, will you destroy and uncreate it all? Right and Wrong, Good and Bad, POD and POC, All 9, Shorts, Boys, and Beyonds.

This applies to relationships. If you are in relationship and you do not expect it to change, you are out of it. The end of the relationship has already occurred; you just have not recognized it.

I was working with a woman who was unhappy in her marriage. I asked her, "How long have you been married?"

She answered, "Far too long."

I asked, "Who are you torturing, him or you?"

She laughed and said, "Both of us! Until you asked me that, I never acknowledged how much I enjoy torturing him. It makes me giggle to torture him and it pisses me off that I torture me. Where is choosing *me* if I stay in that situation just to torture somebody else?"

I said, "You have to look for a different possibility. Ask: 'Do I really need to torture him? Do I really need to torture *me*? Or is there a different possibility?'"

Is there a different possibility?

HOLDING ONTO THINGS

Gary:

Once, when we were talking about change and moving at the speed of space, someone asked about hoarding. Hoarding and holding onto things are a great example of slowing things down so you can believe you are going to create from the things you have hoarded—but that is not actual creation.

Dain:

Energetically, the things you hoard are an anchor that keeps you from changing or moving forward. I grew up around somebody who was a hoarder of magnitude. There was stuff everywhere. They would never let it go. It was "Oh no, I might use that sometime."

As a kid I too had a ton of stuff I thought I might use someday. I hated that stuff and I wanted to get rid of it, but I was never educated about what to do or how to be with something to see if it would contribute in the future. I didn't even know how to ask that question. I didn't have a clue about how to get awareness of what it was to know what to do with all of these things.

Gary:

The idea is "I might need that." Most men have a box or a drawer or a bunch of jars full of screws that they will move from house to house for decades because they might need one of those screws one day. These guys will spend hours going through each one of the screws in the jar to find one they can use. The fact is that it costs them as much in time and energy to hold onto them as it does to drive to the store and get a new one that fits the job exactly.

People do that with their ideals too. They do it with clothes; they do that with all kinds of stuff. If all of those screws, clothes, and other things had their choice, they would choose to move on. They do not want to be hoarded. All you have to do is ask things: "Do you want to stay with me? Or do you want to own somebody else?" That's it. They'll let you know.

When Hurricane Andrew hit Florida, there was a guy on television who was standing by the slab where his house used to be. He said, "I moved down here from Iowa to get away from the tornadoes. I brought all my worldly goods with me. And now all I have is a slab and me." In the end, that is all you get: You.

If you were truly committed to you and your life and you lost everything, it would be "Okay, what's next? What is possible now?" It would not be "Oh my God! I've lost everything."

You think you will not *have* if you let go of things. You try to hold on to what is valuable to you or what you desire to have in your life. Have you ever noticed that when you get rid of all the clothes in your closet that you've been keeping because some day they are going to fit you or come back into style, you suddenly feel a sense of relief? Or when you get rid of a husband or a wife that you do not really want to be with, you feel a sense of relief? Those are places where you open the doors to possibility. Getting rid of stuff opens a door to possibilities.

Getting rid of stuff opens a door to possibilities.

YOU HOARD POINTS OF VIEW, TOO

Gary:

Once when we were talking about hoarding in a class, someone told me her mother was such a hoarder that when the kids went into the house to sweep and clean up, they found grocery bags full of dust bunnies—and the mother wouldn't let the kids throw them away.

Someone else said, "I am holding on to a lot of things that I did not create. Is that hoarding?"

I said, "Yes, that is hoarding. It's what you do with points of view. You take on a point of view because somebody sold you on it. Then you hold onto it because you figure it must have some value. Nobody would give you a point of view that had no value, right? Or would they? Would all kinds of people give you points of view that have no value?"

Whatever you have decided, you have to hoard in order to make sure you can keep your life as slow as everybody else's. Decisions, limitations, other people's points of view, judgments—you are hoarding all those things. You think it is creation, but it is not. Everything that is, will you destroy and uncreate all of that? Right and Wrong, Good and Bad, POD and POC, All 9, Shorts, Boys, and Beyonds.

You think you will not *have* if you let go of things, but hoarding is *holding on* to something; it is not *having* it. You think that holding onto stuff is a great way to have shit. You think that is *having*. It's not. *Having* is not holding onto anything. *True having* is the ability to have—or not have—anything at will.

**True having is the ability to have—
or not have—anything at will.**

SLOWING YOURSELF DOWN

Dain:

When we function from infinite possibilities, we have way more energy available. When we are tired, it's from the limitations we are imposing on ourselves, limitations that we make real—but they do not have to be real and true.

Gary:

My grandson has been staying with Dain and me for the past few weeks, and he does not want to go to bed as long as anyone else is still awake. He says, "I am not tired. I am not tired. I am not tired. I swear I am not tired." He is exhausted.

Dain:

As long as someone is doing something fun and interesting, he is awake. His point of view is "Why would I go to sleep when the world is still awake?"

Gary:

Have you been trying to put yourself to sleep when your world is wide awake? Everything that is times a godzillion, will you destroy and uncreate it all? Right and Wrong, Good and Bad, POD and POC, All 9, Shorts, Boys, and Beyonds.

At one point a while ago I was saying, "I am so tired I do not think I will recover."

Dain asked, "What are you tired of?"

I said, "Stupid people." We POD and POCed that, and he asked, "What are you tired of?"

I said, "The fact that I have to deal with stupid problems that are actually not problems for everybody under the sun who thinks they have a problem. What I'm tired of is everybody wanting me to solve their problems. I couldn't solve their problems anyway, because they don't actually want their problems solved; they just want me to change something and make it easier. They do not want a solution because they could do that in a frigging heartbeat. They just want to feel better about the fact that they have a problem. This is the reason psychologists stay in business forever and never accomplish anything that makes them happy."

Dain said, "Destroy and uncreate all that. What are you tired of?"

I said, "I am tired of the fact that people continually create their limitations as greater and more important than their reality and possibility."

Dain said, "Destroy and uncreate all that. What else are you tired of?"

I said, "I am tired of the fact that nobody seems to want to get greater." We went on like this for a long time.

Dain:

Seriously, it lasted for about a day and a half. Gary kept running it on himself when I was not there. All of sudden he said, "Wow, I am not nearly as tired as I was a day and a half ago!"

Gary:

When you try to make something real for you that is not inherently real for you as a being, you create great tiredness because you have to stop yourself, limit yourself, and slow yourself down enough to pretend that what you are doing is true for you. When you are willing to be the space of possibilities that you truly are, you see that all the stuff you're pretending is not true. It dissolves in the presence of the speed of space that you are.

How many things are you tired of that have nothing to do with anything other than making your body tired? Everything that is times a godzillion, will you destroy and uncreate it, please? Right and Wrong, Good and Bad, POD and POC, All 9, Shorts, Boys, and Beyonds.

When we talk about generation and creation, we are talking about the place where we're capable of the energy of awareness. It's "Wow, something else is possible. How can I use this? How can I do this?"

It's not: "What's wrong with me that I can't do this?"

Gary:

Possibilities create possibilities, which interact with more possibilities. People who have possibilities will create more with you and for you. They will contribute more to you than anything else in life.

Dain:

If you are with Gary for even a moment, you perceive his willingness to have possibilities. It's the space in which he functions. And because he is willing to have possibilities anywhere, possibilities exist.

When you are willing to be the space of possibilities that you truly are, you see that all the stuff you're pretending is not true.

It dissolves in the presence of the speed of space that you are.

11
Creating Money with Greater Ease

Gary:

I was talking with someone who said, "I'm retired and I just recognized that I'm not creating more money because I decided that when life stops being fun, I'll just put my affairs in order and walk out of this body. I'm not creating more money because I decided that my back door is the finiteness of my IRA account."

I said, "Yeah, everyone knows that once you retire you're not allowed to make money. *Retire* means to 'remove oneself from an active reality and an active life.' I'm sorry to say that doesn't fit you. You don't wear retirement well. Would you like to come out of retirement—and start creating your life?"

When I left Santa Barbara and moved to Houston, people said, "You're old enough. You should retire now."

I said, "I'm not old enough to ever retire. I ain't retiring. That's not going to happen. I'm going until I drop dead or fall off my horse on my head."

Would you like to come out of retirement— and start creating your life?

THERE ARE THOUSANDS OF WAYS TO MAKE MONEY

Gary:

How many different ways can you make money? They are infinite, but most people say, "Well, I can do this, I can do this, and I can do this." I ask, "That's all you've got?"

I could make money doing a lemonade stand. There are thousands of ways to make money, but we create limitations and stop ourselves when we begin to define things. We define what we've done in the past as the way to make money.

Dain:

Or we define what somebody else has done as the way to make money. People who don't do definitions make lots of money in all kinds of weird and wonderful ways.

Gary:

How do we *not* make money? I'll tell you: We say, "Hey, I'd like to have more money." The universe says, "Okay, here's a possibility." We say, "No, I won't do that. It doesn't match what I have decided is my way of getting money."

When the possibilities show up and you're not committed to your life, you reject what is offered to you by the universe. You have to reject what the universe offers when you are not committed to your life.

When you *are* committed to your life, you have the possibility of choosing it. This doesn't mean you have to do it. When you're committed to your life, there is nothing you have to do anymore. There is no more *have to* in life.

When you commit to your life, you start creating money in the strangest ways. And all kinds of stuff shows up and you ask, "How the hell did that happen?"

There are thousands of ways to make money, but we create limitations and stop ourselves when we begin to define things.

THE ENERGY OF CREATION

Gary:

One of the things I committed to was using my money to make money, and when you are committed to using your money to make money, possibilities show up with clarity. There is always another possibility. And another. And then you have to make choices.

Everything is available to you if you realize all things are possible. Everything in life is a possibility. Recently, a guy called to ask if I'd be interested in buying a beautiful ebony piano for $5,000. It originally cost $12,000. That is a possibility to make some money. He also offered me three matching crystal chandeliers at a very reasonable price, and we have a client in Australia who wants a matched pair of chandeliers. It's very rare to find matching chandeliers. Will I buy them? Most likely. You have to look at everything that is offered to you and the possibilities that occur.

The energy of creation is not: "What do I need? What do I require? What is going to make this work?" It is not about looking at what you've got to create from. The energy of creation is about looking at what is available that you have not chosen yet.

Possibilities create possibilities, which interact with more possibilities. People who have possibilities will create more with you and for you. They will contribute more to you than anything else in life.

The energy of creation is about looking at what is available that you have not chosen yet.

SPENDING MONEY

Gary:

Dain and I were talking with a friend. She said, "I keep choosing to spend all of my money."

I asked, "Why would you not use your money to create more money instead of just spending it? Who are you trying to be? This is a question you might ask yourself: 'Who am I being with the money I am spending?'"

My friend said, "Oh! I am being my mother! Every time someone talks about how to create money, I feel like an angry, defensive four-year-old."

I said, "When you are four years old, you do not recognize that you are picking up on your mother's stuff. Then as you become a teenager, your parents have had years to build money and they may spend and spend. You see that and you think, "I want to be able to do that." But you need to build money before you can spend it. Get the idea of using your money to make money, whatever that looks like for you. And know that it will be different for you than it is for anybody else."

Why would you not use your money to create more money instead of just spending it?

110

"IF I BUY YOU, WILL YOU MAKE ME MONEY?"

Gary:

Before you spend money on something, try asking these questions:

- If I buy you, will you make me money?
- If invest in you, will you make me money?

Have you ever decided that investing in a house or a stock was going to make you a lot of money? But did it? If you ask the investment or the house or whatever it is a question and listen to its answer, you will always know whether it will make money for you. Ask, "If I buy you, are you going to make me money?" If you get a yes, it will make you money.

Ask this question of anything you are thinking about buying. When you do this, you have to put your beliefs and desires aside so you can receive the answer that is coming to you from the thing you are considering purchasing. If you have a strong conviction that an object, let's say a suit, will make you money no matter what, you're not going to hear the suit's answer. You're not actually asking it, "If I buy you, will you make me money?" But if you ask the suit and truly listen for its answer, it will tell you yes or no. Nothing lies—except you. Things do not lie. This means you can ask them questions, and they will give you the information you request.

If you're thinking about buying a car, ask the car, "Will you make me money?" Will it directly make you money? Not necessarily. This does not always play out in a direct line. The energy of each thing you purchase contributes to the energy of the whole. The energy of the whole then generates the money you would like to have. The car may be the way you get someplace where you will make money.

Asking these questions is not about trying to come to a conclusion about *how* the thing is going to make you money. It's the willingness to have the awareness about *whether* it's going to make you money.

I use this question with everything I consider buying, including my horses, my antiques, my clothes, even my underwear. I am willing to look at everything as contributing to my life. The more you are willing to allow things to contribute to your life and to gift to you whatever energy they have available, the more you can receive—and the more money you can have.

Creating money is different for each one of us. It is not about getting someone else's point of view and going ahead with that. It is about asking how you can create the money you would like to have in your life. Ask: "What are the infinite possibilities of creating money with total ease?" That is a real question. It's not: "What are the infinite possibilities of having a $100,000?" That is not infinite; it's finite!

Did you read the question: "What are the infinite possibilities of creating money with total ease?" without going to "What do I have to *do* to get the money?" People have the point of view that making money is a *doing*, not a *possibility*. The thing that money gives you is the possibility of greater choices. Money does not create energy; it's not an energy bomb. It does not drive your car. It just gives you more choices and more possibility. So how can you create more money with greater ease?

The more you are willing to allow things to contribute to your life and to gift to you whatever energy they have available, the more you can receive—and the more money you can have.

"IF MONEY WASN'T THE ISSUE, WHICH ONE WOULD YOU CHOOSE?"

Gary:

Once Dain and I went out to get a new printer for his office. He found one and said, "This one is the biggest and the best."

Dain:

It was an all-in-one printer for $500.

Gary:

I asked, "If money wasn't the issue, which one would you choose?"

Dain:

I said, "I'd always choose the best." Then I saw that I was making the money the issue. I wasn't looking at which printer would work the best for me. I was saying, "I would choose the best and the most expensive one." So Gary and I had a conversation and I looked around a little bit more. Right around the corner, there was a smaller printer for $150.

Gary:

It did all the things he needed, and it did not have all the bells and whistles that he would not use.

Dain:

And it was half the size. I took home my little $150 baby and I said, "Oh sweet little thing, it's so nice to have you." The other one would not have fit in the place I had available for my printer. It was awesome that Gary asked me that question; otherwise, I would have gotten the big one because it was "the best."

Gary:

And he would have had to take it back because it didn't fit in his office.

Dain:

If money isn't the issue, you can choose what will work best for you that you are not willing to look at or willing to receive the awareness of.

Gary:

It is not about being able to afford the best and the most. It is about being aware of how something will actually work for you. You have ask: "What it is going to create?"

> *If money isn't the issue, you can choose what*
> *will work best for you that you are not willing*
> *to look at or receive the awareness of.*

MONEY IS JUST THE POSSIBILITY

Gary:

When you're owned by money, you always think money is the answer. When you're not owned by money, money is never the answer; it's just the possibility.

Most people are unwilling to be owned by money, but they *are* willing to be owned by the lack thereof. When you say, "I do not have enough money," you are owned by money. You don't ask:

- How can I create this without money?
- How can I do this anyway?

Dain:

When we found the property for the center we are building in Costa Rica, we did not have an extra four and a half million dollars sitting around anywhere to pay for it. We didn't say, "Well, since we do not have the money, we cannot create the center." We asked, "How can we create it?" That stimulated a whole new conversation.

Gary:

It doesn't matter whether you have money or you don't have money; you can still be owned by money. You think you have to control everything to make sure you have money so you are able to continue to not own your life and not be owned by money. The amount of effort and time it takes you to think about money and work with money and deal with money! If it takes you more than two and a half minutes to decide whether you are going to buy something, you are owned by money.

> *"What are the infinite possibilities of creating money with total ease?"*

ARE YOU OWNED BY YOUR CHEAPNESS?

Gary:

I was talking with someone who got into a messy complication with an airline because she was trying to book the cheapest seat she could find. She thought the airline was creating the complication. I said, "You know, it was your search for the cheapest seat that made this complicated. It might be easier to buy another ticket, upgrade, or go to a different airline. You are owned by your cheapness."

She said, "Thank you so much for that! It's the legacy of my family."

If you are owned by your cheapness, would you like to give that up now? Everything that is times a godzillion, will you destroy and uncreate it all? Right and Wrong, Good and Bad, POD and POC, All 9, Shorts, Boys, and Beyonds.

Someone else said, "My sister inherited a huge amount of money. She's a millionaire—and she clips coupons every Sunday." Being cheap is not the way you become a millionaire. She inherited a lot of money; she did not create it.

Dain:

Interesting, because a lot of people who inherit money do the exact opposite. They blow through their inheritance and spend it all. They end up in the same place as the woman who was clipping coupons. She has the money but she does not actually *have* the money. She does not have access to the money; she does not have the freedom of the money.

Gary:

She is still owned by her poverty.

When you're being cheap, you're functioning from the point of view that what you have is going to run out. You try to create as little as possible or to desire or need as little as possible. You think that if you use less, you'll slow down the process of running out. What you don't realize is you slow down everything else as well.

Dain:

Yeah, not creating definitely does not create millions. Could it be that being creative could create millions? What if you were willing to create more?

> **If you are owned by your cheapness,
> would you like to give that up now?**

THE COMEDY OF THE ABSURD WITH MONEY

Gary:

A lady told me about her father's last day. He had been diagnosed with cancer and was in his bed. He said to her, "Do you know what I'm craving? A cream puff. I love cream puffs but I haven't had one for ten years because they used to be twenty-five cents then they went up to $2.50, and I refused to buy them anymore because they were too expensive."

The woman said, "My dad's universe revolved around money. He was a hoarder. He never paid a dime of taxes. He never kept a job. He denied himself a cream puff for ten years because they cost $2.50. And that was the last thing he ate. The silliness of not having or creating what you desire and limiting yourself around money is ridiculous."

It is the comedy of the absurd.

Dain:

What have you made so vital about living the comedy of the absurd with money that is not your reality? Everything that is times a godzillion, will you destroy and uncreate it all? Right and Wrong, Good and Bad, POD and POC, All 9, Shorts, Boys, and Beyonds.

> **What have you made so vital about living the comedy of the absurd with money that is not your reality?**

12
Pretense and Illusion versus Awareness

Gary:

I recently had a conversation with one of the people who works for us. He said, "I am only making x amount of money. I am not being a very big contribution to my mate."

I asked, "Are you sure? How much are you actually making per month? Would you please add up all the money you made last month and the month before?" So he added everything up and said, "Oh my God! I made twice as much as I thought I made. I was not willing to have the awareness of my increase of possibilities."

He could make himself wrong as long as he never looked at what was true. Is this something you do? As long as you never look at what is true, you can make yourself wrong. You can keep yourself diminished. You have to be willing to look at what is actually true. Ask:

- What is actually true for me?
- What is true here?

Some people won't do this because they think it is more fun to get caught up in emotions, because everyone knows emotions are way more fun than possibilities.

As long as you never look at what is true, you can make yourself wrong.

You can keep yourself diminished.

You have to be willing to look at what is actually true.

NO PRETENSE

Gary:

What would happen if you saw what was true for you? What are you capable of that you are not acknowledging? What are you pretending is true for you that is not? You have to realize what is real for you. The greatest difficulty in life is to be honest with yourself.

You say, "I am going to become a physicist, but I do not know math. Well, that is all right, I can cope." The pretense is "I want to be it; therefore, I can be it."

If you have bought the point of view that you are not good at math, how can you have the awareness of what you can choose? You could be a physicist if you were good at math but if you are not good at math, how can you choose to be a physicist? You can either function from the illusion that *you are bad* or you can function from the illusion that *you can have*. Actually, all you have to do is ask: "What would I have to choose different to create being a physicist as a possibility?" There is no pretense in that.

If you say, "Okay, I am not good at math, but this is what I want to do and be," you will go out and create it. But if you talk about it and you do not create it, it's because you do not really want to do it.

**What are you capable of that you
are not acknowledging?**

JUST GET TO FRIGGING WORK!

Gary:

People tell me, "I am going to do this," and then I see them not doing it. They are buying into the pretense that possibility is not real. They don't ask: "What is actually possible for me that I have not chosen yet?"

Dain:

When you are honest with yourself, the greatest difficulty in life is to be in the presence of those who are doing extreme pretense.

Gary:

I was talking with someone who said she desired to be an artist. She went on and on about her expectations of being that. I said, "Stop! This is the most boring story I've ever heard in my life. Could you find any more ways to stop yourself? If you want to be an artist, just get to frigging work! What do you need to do?"

What would you like to be that you've never become? I'm going to give you a hint. Here's one step that will get you there: Get out of bed. All you have to do is get up in the morning and go to it. You keep saying, "I want to be this but I can't do it because I have this and I don't have that." If you really want to be something, just do it! Be it. Get out of bed and start moving. You're not going to get there by playing around at it. You get there by actually choosing it.

> **You buy into the pretense that possibility is not real.**

> **You don't ask: "What is actually possible for me that I have not chosen yet?**

DOES LIFE HAVE TO BE HARD?

Gary:

Have you been buying the pretense that life has to be hard—that your life cannot be easy?

Your life is not hard; your life is easy, but instead of recognizing "My life is easy," you try to make it hard. You are trying to prove a lie you bought from somebody else. Life for you is easy. Why do you make that wrong?

People tell me, "My life is so hard. You do not know how bad it is."

I say, "Your life ain't that hard. It ain't that difficult. Get over it and move on." Nobody cares how bad your life is. Do you get that? Do you have to create a disability in order to prove you are having a hard life? How is that working for you?

What is wrong with "My life is too frigging easy and it is going to get easier"? That is creating from possibilities.

> **Have you been buying the pretense that life has to be hard—that your life cannot be easy?**

TRAUMA AND DRAMA

Gary:

You have awareness—yet you buy the idea that unawareness is more real. Unawareness is more real than awareness? Talk about a comedy of the absurd! That is a comedy, but you create it as a tragedy. I ask, "Why do you create your life as a tragedy?"

People say, "But I have lost so much. You do not understand..." I say, "Yes, I do understand, and I still think you are absurd." Or they say, "I had a great relationship and now it is gone." I say, "Good riddance to bad rubbish."

"You do not understand" is the funniest thing anybody could ever say to me.

What have you made so vital about living the comedy of the absurd as not your reality when it is your reality so that you can pretend that you are as screwed up as you have decided you are or should be? Everything that is times a godzillion, will you destroy and uncreate it all? Right and Wrong, Good and Bad, POD and POC, All 9, Shorts, Boys, and Beyonds.

Speaking of the comedy of the absurd, at one point many years ago, my ex-wife and I were having a giant argument. I looked at my son and I said, "Pack your bags. We are leaving," because we all know leaving is the greatest threat you can make.

My son said, "I don't have any bags, Dad."

I said, "Then get some grocery bags." That kind of broke the mood because it is hard to be serious when your kid has to get grocery bags so you can leave in the elegant "I am leaving" style.

I said, "Okay, never mind. I am over my point of view." I got how absurd I was being.

Have you ever done that type of trauma and drama in your life? It is the comedy of the absurd. Are you unwilling to recognize when you are creating the comedy of the absurd you call your life? Until you really commit to your reality and to your life, you cannot change this.

What have you made so vital about living the comedy of the absurd as not your reality when it is your reality so that you can pretend you are as screwed up as you have decided you are or decided you should be? Everything that is times a godzillion, will you destroy and uncreate it all? Right and Wrong, Good and Bad, POD and POC, All 9, Shorts, Boys, and Beyonds.

> *You have awareness—yet you buy
> that unawareness is more real.*
>
> **Talk about a comedy of the absurd!**

DO YOU THINK IT'S MORE FUN TO BELIEVE THAN TO BE AWARE?

Gary:

I met with a guy the other day who is a high-powered attorney. I said, "Your problem is that you believe what people say instead of hearing what is in their head. If they say the right things, you assume they are going to follow through on what they said. You are not willing to look at people and ask, 'Who is a liar?' I always ask, 'Who is a liar?'"

When you are committed to your own life you know what is true for you and as a result, you know when people are lying. You don't have to address the lie. You just say to yourself, "Okay, here's a liar. What can I trust? I can trust that this person will lie, not that what they say is going to happen."

Are you committed to your awareness or not? Most people are committed to believing in illusions. They think it's more fun to *believe* than it is to *be aware*.

Do people lie to *you* or do they lie to *themselves*? Both. So why would you believe what comes out of someone's mouth? If they are talking, they are lying. It's not a rightness or a wrongness; it's just what they do. It's what they choose.

Here's what it boils down to: Does that lie create infinite possibilities or finite possibilities? Finite. What do you want to live from—infinite possibilities or finite possibilities? If you want to live from infinite possibilities, give up your belief in belief. Never believe, always question. When you question, things change.

What have you made so vital about being in absolute opposition and resistance to infinite possibilities that keeps you living in the finite pile of shit this reality creates as your life? Everything that is times a godzillion, will you destroy and uncreate it, please? Right and Wrong, Good and Bad, POD and POC, All 9, Shorts, Boys, and Beyonds.

***If you want to live from infinite possibilities,
give up your belief in belief.***

***Never believe, always question.
When you question, things change.***

13
The Fire-Breathing Dragon of Possibility Called You

Gary:

People have the idea that there is *home*, a place where you belong. That's a lie. There is no such place as home. What if home was not about the *place* where you belong but the *space* that you are? The only real home is being *you*.

Dain:

When I lived in Santa Barbara, it felt like home to me. I loved the space of nature. Then we moved. For the first nine months we lived in Houston, I hated it. Then one day I said, "Wait a minute. What is the space that I can create as my home, here and now?" I got that home is the space you choose to be and create. I am usually home anywhere I am because I know that home is the space you are willing to be.

Gary:

The only real home is being *you*. Everywhere where you have defined *home* as a *place* instead of the *space of being*, will you destroy and uncreate all that? Right and Wrong, Good and Bad, POD and POC, All 9, Shorts, Boys, and Beyonds.

127

You are a gypsy of consciousness. If you had a caravan, if you had a horse with a cart where you could live, you would be happier than if you had a place called home. Of course, you would have to have indoor plumbing.

Dain:

Gary and I travel almost continuously, doing Access classes around the world. People ask us, "How do you travel so much? Don't you hate it?" We say, "No, we love it. We love the fact that in the next two months we will be in six different places and three different countries and eight different hotels. It works for us."

How can you create your life so it works for you to live as the home of infinite possibilities wherever you are? I'm just asking. It's just a thought. Just a possibility.

How can you create your life so it actually works rather than resisting the fact that you have a home?

Gary:

Everywhere where you call home is a limitation. Would an infinite being have a home? Or would an infinite being be home everywhere? *Home* is a construct we create in order to have a place where we belong instead of being the space that creates.

A lady told us, "When I was little, we moved a lot. My dad was drinking and my mom would pack us all up and move us around. She used to say to my brother and me, 'Home is where we are.'"

I said to her, "No, home is not where you are. Home is what you *is*."

She said, "Oh! Thank you. That has a different energy."

Gary:

Home is what you *is*. It's an East Texan thing to say: "Home is what you *is*."

What have you defined as home that actually isn't? Everything that is times a godzillion, will you destroy and uncreate it? Right and Wrong, Good and Bad, POD and POC, All 9, Shorts, Boys, and Beyonds.

The only real home is being you.

BECOMING A CATALYST FOR CHANGE

Gary:

What if you came here to be a catalyst for change for the world? Are you choosing that? Or are you just trying to fit in? Are you trying to be normal? Are you trying to be like other people? Do you get that you may be highly committed to the limitations of your life? Is that your primary commitment—to how limited and screwed up you are?

If you do not choose what is possible, how are you going to change the world?

Your commitment could be the change you are for the world. Are you willing to commit to being somebody who changes the world? By the way, one person can change the world. How many people can you change by a choice you can make?

Dain:

It is time for all of us to step up and be the leaders that we are.

Gary:

You know somewhere that you came here to change the world. Start looking for the infinite possibilities of how you can change it. Ask: "What are the infinite possibilities of changing the world?"

Something different is going to show up, and it may not look like anything you thought you were going to choose or do.

Stop trying to choose what is "right" or what fulfills some dream you have. Stop trying to choose what makes other people happy or proud. See that you have capacities. You have possibilities. You have things you have not chosen. What if you chose for everything you really wanted?

Be what you are. You have a possibility. You have a choice. Ask: "What do I have available that nobody else does?"

Dain:

If you do not choose what is possible, who is going to choose it? Everything you have decided the home of infinite possibilities is that it is not, and all of the projections, expectations, separations, judgments, and rejections that are yours or somebody else's, and everywhere you are saying, "But this is not what I decided it would be," will you destroy and uncreate that, please? Right and Wrong, Good and Bad, POD and POC, All 9, Shorts, Boys, and Beyonds.

Gary:

What would you have to acknowledge about you that you've never acknowledged that if you would acknowledge it would give you the ability to commit to your own life and create infinite possibilities? Everything that is times a godzillion, will you destroy and uncreate it all? Right and Wrong, Good and Bad, POD and POC, All 9, Shorts, Boys, and Beyonds?

What would you have to acknowledge about you that you've never acknowledged that if you would acknowledge it would give you the ability to commit to your own life and create infinite possibilities?

THE FIRE-BREATHING DRAGON OF POSSIBILITY

Gary:

When a participant in the Home of Infinite Possibilities class heard that clearing, she said, "When I put my awareness on that clearing, it's like 'Oh shit. Something is occurring. I'm about to be consumed by this because it's so huge.'"

We then had a conversation that went like this:

Dain:

Let it in, baby!

Gary:

You mean you could be consumed by owning you?

Class Participant:

It feels like annihilation, like death.

Dain:

You are correct. It is the death of the stupid *you.*

Class Participant:

How do I open to that when it feels so frigging intense?

Dain:

Just enjoy it. You are being burned alive by possibilities.

Class Participant:

It's huge.

Dain:

Oh, it's bigger than that.

Class Participant:

There are no words to contain it.

Dain:

Stop trying to contain it.

Gary:

Can I ask you a question? Have you wanted to change the world?

Class Participant:

Yes!

Gary:

Well, choose that, and you will.

Dain:

It is right there. Breathe it in, baby. It's in your ear saying, "I am here! Ha-ha-ha!"

Gary:

That's very funny. I got the image of the fire-breathing dragon of possibility, and you are saying, "No! Go away! Go away! You could kill me!" If you become a dragon, you won't have a problem with winter any longer. You can just ask your body to adjust. You can say, "Make me as hot as I really am."

What have you made so vital about avoiding the fire-breathing dragon of possibility called *you* that keeps you from enjoying the infinite possibilities that you would create in the world and change all reality with? Everything that is times a godzillion, will you destroy and uncreate it all? Right and Wrong, Good and Bad, POD and POC, All 9, Shorts, Boys, and Beyonds.

Class Participant:

That is how it feels. It's so intense.

Dain:

You've been taught by this reality that anything so intense is bad and it will annihilate you.

Gary:

Everything you've done to not be as intense as you actually are, will you destroy and uncreate it? "You're just a little too much." The moment you get to "a little too much" is when you're just about to be enough. Right and Wrong, Good and Bad, POD and POC, All 9, Shorts, Boys, and Beyonds.

What have you made so vital about avoiding the fire-breathing dragon of possibility called *you* that keeps you from enjoying the infinite possibilities you would create in the world and change all reality with? Everything that is times a godzillion, will you destroy and uncreate it all? Right and Wrong, Good and Bad, POD and POC, All 9, Shorts, Boys, and Beyonds.

Class Participant:

I woke up out of a dream at 3:45 this morning, and it came to me that commitment to my life is being all in. There's no sitting on the fence; there's no poking one toe in. It's your whole body. It's balls to the wall. It's applying the Access tools when you're getting tripped up or whatever your bullshit story is. It's choosing total awareness and just going for it.

Gary:

Awesome. Thank you.

Dain:

What have you made so vital about avoiding the fire-breathing dragon of possibility called *you* that keeps you from enjoying the infinite possibilities you would create in the world and change all reality with by committing to your life? Everything that is times a godzillion, will you destroy and uncreate it all? Right and Wrong, Good and Bad, POD and POC, All 9, Shorts, Boys, and Beyonds.

Who tells a dragon where to go? No one. The dragon tells the dragon where to go, and the dragon goes wherever the dragon wants to go. Because if there is not a path, he breathes fire and creates one.

What have you made so vital about avoiding the fire-breathing dragon of possibility called *you* that keeps you from enjoying the infinite possibilities you would create in the world and change all reality with by committing to your life? Everything that is times a godzillion, will you destroy and uncreate it all? Right and Wrong, Good and Bad, POD and POC, All 9, Shorts, Boys, and Beyonds.

Class Participant:

You said that when you commit to your life, you are choosing to change everything. That was huge. The commitment to your life will open everything up because you're willing to be anything.

Gary:

When you commit to your life, you get to see what doesn't work. You know when something isn't working, and you say, "Okay, I'm out of here. I'm not doing this." When you commit to your own life, you can be, do, have, create, or generate anything and everything at choice and at will.

> **When you commit to your own life, you can be, do, have, create, or generate anything and everything at choice and at will.**

WHEN YOU COMMIT TO YOUR LIFE, YOU GET TO BE YOU

Gary:

After that conversation, some other class participants joined in:

Class Participant:

I have been perpetrating on myself the idea that I am *subject* to my life instead of I get to *create* my life. I get it now. When I commit to my life, I get to be me. I get to be in this body. I get to have this awareness. I get to do all these cool things.

Dain:

That changes everything, because rather than asking, "Oh! Why am I me? Why did I come to this family? Why did I have these parents? Why did I experience this abuse? Why did I come in without billions of dollars? Why do I have this? Why do I have that? Why do I have these relationships?" you say, "Hey! I get to be me!"

Class Participant:

Yes, I get to be me!

Gary:

If you are talking about trying to identify *you*, there is nothing there that is called *you*.

Dain:

There is nothing that is solid enough to be called *you*.

Gary:

When you recognize that, it lets you go here and go there. It creates this possibility and opens that door. Everything you have ever done in your life got you to where you are today. Every choice you made got you to where you are today. And because of that, you have a different set of choices.

Dain:

Have you noticed how baby dragons breathe out little puffs of smoke because they don't know how to breathe fire yet? I have a big sense of the possibility of having some intense dragon playmates while walking on this planet.

Gary:

All you baby dragons, will you at least commit to being the dragon-ass you really are instead of draggin' your ass around the planet? Everything that is times a godzillion, will you destroy and uncreate it all? Right and Wrong, Good and Bad, POD and POC, All 9, Shorts, Boys, and Beyonds.

What is required for you to shift and change? What proof of finiteness are you using to create the limitations you are choosing?

What have you made so vital about avoiding the fire-breathing dragon of possibility called *you* that keeps you from enjoying the infinite possibilities you would create in the world and change all reality with by committing to your life? Everything that is times a godzillion, will you destroy and uncreate it all?

Right and Wrong, Good and Bad, POD and POC, All 9, Shorts, Boys, and Beyonds.

Class Participant:

I had a revelation of the greatness of me, and I let it go by without committing. Does an infinite being get infinite chances to commit?

Gary:

Yeah, it's called whenever you frigging want to get to it.

Who and what are you that you claim not to be that if you would be it would give you all of you and infinite possibilities? Everything that is times a godzillion, will you destroy and uncreate it all? Right and Wrong, Good and Bad, POD and POC, All 9, Shorts, Boys, and Beyonds.

Class Participant:

When you actually commit to your life, your life is way bigger than just you. It's about connecting to everything. It's being the Kingdom of We. You choose for *you* and *everybody* else.

Gary:

You have a gift called "I'm able to create." Look at your life. Look at what you have created. Has it been awful? Has it been good? Could it be greater? Yes, but it's only going to get greater if you commit your life. Home is what you *is*. What if what you are, what you can be, and what you can create is you as a gift?

What if what you are, what you can be, and what you can create is you as a gift?

WHAT DO YOU CHOOSE?

Gary:

You have the tools, the pathway, the capacity, the invitation, and the inspiration to not only commit to your life but to step into it and be present in a way that has never been available before. You can use these things as a springboard.

Please know that it never feels or looks the way you think it's going to look or feel. Whatever breakthrough you have is the breakthrough you require. When you have it, there are not going to be any clouds that part, there will not be a deep voice that speaks to you, nor will there be angels who play music. All you require might be a choice that is like a whisper.

You are now choosing your life. It's that simple. It might be "Oh, cool. I have a different choice." Half the time you'll miss it. You won't recognize it until six months later. If you are new to Access, you might say, "Yeah, I heard what you said, but where is my formula? Where's my answer?" I have to tell you there is no formula and there is no answer. There is only choice. What do you choose?

There is no formula and there is no answer. There is only choice.

What do you choose?

The Access Consciousness Clearing Statement®

*You are the only one who can unlock the
points of view that have you trapped.*

*What we are offering with the clearing
process is a tool you can use
to change the energy of the points of view that
have you locked into unchanging situations.*

Throughout this book, we ask a lot of questions, and some of those questions might twist your head around a little bit. That's our intention. The questions are designed to get your mind out of the picture so you can get to the *energy* of a situation.

Once the question has twisted your head around and brought up the energy of a situation, we'll ask if you are willing to destroy and uncreate that energy—because stuck energy is the source of barriers and limitations. Destroying and uncreating that energy will open the door to new possibilities for you.

This is your opportunity to say, "Yes, I'm willing to let go of whatever is holding that limitation in place."

That will be followed by some weird-speak we call the clearing statement:

Right and Wrong, Good and Bad, POD and POC, All 9, Shorts, Boys, and Beyonds.

With the clearing statement, we're going back to the energy of the limitations and barriers that have been created. We're looking at the energies that keep us from moving forward and expanding into all of the spaces that we would like to go. The clearing statement addresses the energies that are creating the limitations and contractions in our life.

The more you run the clearing statement, the deeper it goes and the more layers and levels it can unlock for you. If a lot of energy comes up for you in response to a question, you may wish to repeat the process numerous times until the subject being addressed is no longer an issue for you.

You don't have to understand the words of the clearing statement for it to work because it's about the energy. However, if you're interested in knowing what the words mean, some brief definitions are given below.

Right and Wrong, Good and Bad is shorthand for: What's right, good, perfect, and correct about this? What's wrong, mean, vicious, terrible, bad, and awful about this? The short version of these questions is: What's right and wrong, good and bad? It is the things that we consider right, good, perfect, and/or correct that stick us the most. We do not wish to let go of them since we decided that we have them right.

POD stands for the **P**oint **o**f **D**estruction; all the ways you have been destroying yourself in order to keep whatever you're clearing in existence.

POC stands for the Point of Creation of the thoughts, feelings, and emotions immediately preceding your decision to lock the energy in place.

Sometimes people say, "POD and POC it," which is shorthand for the longer statement. When you "POD and POC" something, it is like pulling the bottom card out of a house of cards. The whole thing falls down.

All 9 stands for the nine different ways you have created this item as a limitation in your life. They are the layers of thoughts, feelings, emotions, and points of view that create the limitation as solid and real.

Shorts is the short version of a much longer series of questions that include: What's meaningful about this? What's meaningless about this? What's the punishment for this? What's the reward for this?

Boys stands for energetic structures called nucleated spheres. Basically these have to do with those areas of our life where we've tried to handle something continuously with no effect. There are at least thirteen different kinds of these spheres, which are collectively called "the boys." A nucleated sphere looks like the bubbles created when you blow in one of those kids' bubble pipes that has multiple chambers. It creates a huge mass of bubbles, and when you pop one bubble, the other bubbles fill in the space.

Have you ever tried to peel away the layers of an onion when you were trying to get to the core of an issue, but you could never get there? That's because it wasn't an onion; it was a nucleated sphere.

Beyonds are feelings or sensations that stop your heart, stop your breath, or stop your willingness to look at possibilities. Beyonds are what occur when you are in shock. We have lots of areas in our life where we freeze up. Anytime you freeze up, it's a beyond holding you captive. That's the difficulty with a beyond: it stops you from being present. The beyonds include everything that is beyond belief, reality, imagination, conception, perception, rationalization, forgiveness, as well as all the other beyonds. They are usually feelings and sensations, rarely emotions, and never thoughts.